# Jesus Came to Save **Sinners**

*Therefore having overlooked the times of ignorance, God is now declaring to men that all people everywhere should repent.* (Acts 17:30)

# Jesus Came to Save Sinners

## to Save **Sinners**

*An Earnest Conversation with Those*
*Who Long for Salvation and Eternal Life*

CHARLES H. SPURGEON

ANEKO
PRESS

We love hearing from our readers. Please contact us at www.anekopress.com/questions-comments with any questions, comments, or suggestions.

*Jesus Came to Save Sinners* – Charles H. Spurgeon
Updated Edition Copyright © 2017
First edition published 1886
Previously titled *All of Grace*

Unless otherwise indicated, scripture quotations are taken from the New American Standard Bible® (NASB), copyright © 1960, 1962, 1963, 1968, 1971, 1972, 1973, 1975, 1977, 1995 by The Lockman Foundation. Used by permission. www.Lockman.org.

Some scripture quotations are taken from the Jubilee Bible, copyright © 2000, 2001, 2010, 2013 by Russell M. Stendal. Used by permission of Russell M. Stendal, Bogota, Colombia. All rights reserved.

*Cover Design: Natalia Hawthorne*
*Cover Photography: Begun/Shutterstock*
*Editors: Donna Sundblad and Ruth Zetek*

Printed in the United States of America
Aneko Press

www.anekopress.com
Aneko Press, Life Sentence Publishing, and our logos are trademarks of
Life Sentence Publishing, Inc.
203 E. Birch Street
P.O. Box 652
Abbotsford, WI 54405

**RELIGION / Christian Ministry / Evangelism**
Paperback ISBN: 978-1-62245-451-8
eBook ISBN: 978-1-62245-452-5

10  9  8  7  6  5  4  3  2
Available where books are sold

# Contents

*This updated edition is dedicated to the residents of Abbotsford, Wisconsin*

---

# To You

In my efforts to best discuss this most important topic, I've chosen plain and simple language so no matter who reads this book the Holy Spirit can impress them with the truth. And whether educated or uneducated, no matter who reads and is impressed with the truth found in these pages, I pray some might go on to become great winners of souls.

Who knows how many will find their way to peace by what they read? A more important question is: Will you be one of them?

A certain man built a fountain by the side of the road and hung a cup near it by a little chain. Sometime later, a well-known art critic found fault with its design. When told of the criticism the man who built the fountain asked, "Do many thirsty people drink at the fountain?" He was told thousands of poor people, men, women, and children satisfied their thirst at this fountain. He smiled because he wasn't really troubled by the critic's observation. Instead, he only hoped the critic himself might fill the cup some sultry summer's day and be refreshed and praise the name of the Lord.

Here is my fountain, and this is my cup. Find fault if you want, but please drink of the water of life. This is all I really care about. I would rather bless the soul of the rag-gatherer or the poorest of those who sweep a path ahead of people crossing dirty urban streets in exchange for a gratuity, than please a prince from a royal bloodline and fail to convert him to God.

Are you sincere about reading this book? If so, we are agreed from the beginning. My goal is nothing short of your finding Christ and heaven. Oh, how I hope we can seek this together. I do so by dedicating this little book with prayer. Won't you join me by looking up to God and asking Him to bless you while you read it? The foreseeing care and guidance of God has put these pages in your path and while you have a little spare time in which to read them, you are willing to give your time to reading. This is a good sign. Who knows what blessing will come to you for the time you set aside? At any rate, *Today if you hear His voice, do not harden your hearts, as when they provoked Me* (Hebrews 3:15).

**My goal is nothing short of your finding Christ and heaven.**

Introduction

# Where Are You?

I heard a story about a minister who called at the home of a poor woman. He intended to give her financial help, because he knew she was very poor. With his money in his hand, he knocked at the door, but she didn't answer. He decided she wasn't home and went his way. A little while later, he met her at the church and told her he'd remembered her need. "I called at your house and knocked several times," he said. "I supposed you weren't at home, because no one came to the door."

"What time was this, sir?"

"It was about noon."

"Oh dear," she said. "I heard you, and I am so sorry I didn't answer. I thought it was the landlord calling for the rent." Many who are financially struggling understand what this meant.

It is my desire to be heard, and therefore, I want to

say I'm not calling for the rent. Without question, the object of this book isn't to ask anything of you, but to tell you that salvation is totally by grace, which means free, for nothing, without charge.

Often, when we want to gain someone's attention, they tend to think, "Now I'm going to be told what I'm required to do. This man knocking on my door is going to ask me to give what is due to God. But I'm sure I have nothing to pay with so I will pretend to not be at home."

This book isn't like this. It doesn't demand anything from you. Instead, it brings you something. We aren't going to talk about law, duty, and punishment. No, we will talk about love, goodness, forgiveness, mercy, and eternal life. Therefore, don't act like you're not at home – don't turn a deaf ear or a careless heart. I'm asking nothing of you in the name of God or man. It's not my intent to require anything from your hands. Instead, I come in God's name to bring you a free gift which will bring you present and eternal joy when you receive it.

**We will talk about love, goodness, forgiveness, mercy, and eternal life.**

Open the door, and let my sincere pleas enter. Come and let us reason together (Isaiah 1:18). The Lord Himself invites you to meet to discuss your immediate and endless happiness, and He wouldn't do this if He didn't mean well toward you. Don't refuse the Lord Jesus who knocks at your door, because He knocks with a hand which was nailed to the cross for people like you and me. Since His only purpose is your good, draw near and listen carefully to Him. Let the good Word sink into your soul. It may be the time has come for you to enter that new life which is the beginning of heaven. *Faith comes from hearing*, and reading is a sort of hearing (Romans 10:17). Faith may come to you while reading this book. Why not? O blessed Spirit of all grace, make it so.

> *Whosoever drinks of the water that I will*
> *give him shall never thirst; but the water*
> *that I will give him will become in him a*
> *well of water springing up to eternal life.*
> (John 4:14)

# Chapter 1

# God Justifies the Ungodly

This message found in the letter to the Romans is for you. *But to the one who does not work, but believes in Him who justifies the ungodly, his faith is credited as righteousness* (Romans 4:5). I call your attention to these words, *Him who justifies the ungodly*. Aren't you surprised to see such an expression in the Bible – *who justifies the <u>ungodly</u>*?

These words seem incredibly wonderful to me, but I've actually heard people who hate the doctrines of the cross complain against God because He saves wicked men and receives the vilest of the vile to Himself. See how this Scripture clearly accepts the charge. By the mouth of His servant Paul, by the inspiration of the Holy Spirit, He takes on the title of *Him who justifies the ungodly*. He makes those just who are unjust, forgives those who deserve to be punished, and grants grace to those who don't deserve it.

Do you think salvation is only for those who are good? That God's grace is only for the pure and holy who are free from sin? Have you forgotten that if you were spiritually worthy God would reward you? And have you thought that because you are not worthy, there's no way you'll ever enjoy His favor? If that's the case, then you must find it somewhat surprising to read a verse like this: *Him who justifies the ungodly.* It's no wonder you're surprised. Even with all my familiarity with God's great grace, it never ceases to amaze me. It seems astonishing to think a holy God can possibly be willing to justify an unholy person, doesn't it?

According to our natural reliance on works for salvation, we tend to always talk about our own goodness and our own worthiness. We stubbornly hold to the idea that there must be something good in us for God to take notice of us. But this is a deception, and God sees through all deceptions. He knows that there is no goodness whatsoever in us. He says that *there is none righteous, not even one* (Romans 3:10), and He knows *all our righteous deeds are like a filthy garment* (Isaiah 64:6). Therefore, the Lord Jesus didn't come into the world looking for those who were good and righteous, but to grant these virtues to people in need of them. He comes not because we are just, but to make us so, for He is the One *who justifies the ungodly.*

When a lawyer comes into court, if he is an honest man, he desires to plead the case of an innocent person and justify him from his false charges before the court. The lawyer's goal should be to justify the innocent person, and he shouldn't attempt to protect the guilty party. People don't really have the right or the power truly to justify the guilty. This is a miracle reserved for the Lord alone.

God, the infinitely just Sovereign, knows *there is not a righteous man on earth who continually does good and who never sins* (Ecclesiastes 7:20). Therefore, in the infinite sovereignty of His divine nature and the splendor of His indescribable love, He undertakes the task not so much of justifying the just, as of justifying the ungodly (Mark 2:17). God has devised methods and resources of making it possible for the ungodly man to stand justly accepted before Him. With perfect justice, He has set up a system by which He can treat the guilty as if they lived free from offense all their life. In this way, He can treat them as if they are totally free from sin. He *justifies the ungodly*.

> God has set up a system by which He can treat the guilty as if they lived free from offense all their life.

Jesus Christ came into the world to save sinners. It's a very unexpected thing – a thing to be marveled at most of all by those who experience it. Even to this day, to me it is the greatest miracle I've ever heard of that God would justify me. Apart from His almighty love, I feel like I'm a lump of unworthiness, an accumulation of corruption, and a heap of sin.

However, I know without a doubt that I'm justified by faith in Christ Jesus. And because of grace, I'm treated like I've lived perfectly upright, and I'm made an heir of God and a joint heir with Christ. Yet by birth, I must take my place among the most sinful. I'm entirely undeserving, but I'm treated as if I am deserving. I'm loved with the same amount of love as if I've always lived godly, while in times past I was ungodly. Who wouldn't be astonished at this? Gratitude for such kindness stands dressed in robes of wonder. While on one hand this is very surprising, notice how it makes the gospel available to you and me. If God *justifies the ungodly*, then He can justify you. When you look at yourself honestly, isn't that the kind of person you are? If you haven't received grace through faith, you're unconverted, *for by grace you have been saved through faith; and that not of yourselves, it is the gift of God* (Ephesians 2:8). *Ungodly* is a very appropriate description of you, because you've lived without God. You've lived the reverse of godly.

**If you haven't received grace through faith, you're unconverted.**

Perhaps you know a little about God and give lip service to faith in Him, but you don't live for Him. You use His name in vain, you cheat on taxes, or you gossip about others behind their back. Perhaps you are even living in sexual immorality, all the while telling me that you love God.

Or, you may have even doubted God's existence and even confirmed it with your words. You've lived on this beautiful earth full of evidence that makes known God's presence, and all the while, you've shut your eyes to the clear demonstration of His power and godhead. Instead, you've lived as if there is no God, and it would have pleased you if you could have proved to yourself with certainty that He didn't exist. It could be that you have lived in this way for many years and are now pretty well settled in your ways. But God isn't in any of your ways if you fit the label "ungodly." And the label would fit, wouldn't it?

You could possibly be a person of another sort. Perhaps you've regularly taken part in all the outward forms of religion, but your heart isn't in them. Even though you've been meeting with the people of God, you've never met with God yourself on a personal level. You've been in the choir and have praised the Lord with your lips but not with your heart. You've lived without real love for God in your heart or any regard for His commands in your daily life. Instead, you've really lived an ungodly life.

If any of this rings true for you, you're just the kind of person to whom this good news is sent – this gospel which says that God *justifies the ungodly.* This good news is not only wonderful, it is also thankfully available for you. If you are a sensible person, you'll see the remarkable grace of God in His provision for a person like you, and you'll say to yourself, "Justify me, the ungodly! Why shouldn't I be justified and justified immediately?" With all my heart, I wish you would accept it!

The salvation of God is for those who don't deserve it and have no way to make themselves ready or good enough for it. This may sound odd, but it is a reasonable statement because the only ones who need justifying are those who have no justification of their own. That includes all of us. For only the perfectly righteous would have no need of justifying.

You may feel you are fulfilling your religious obligation, and by living this way almost feel like heaven is under an obligation to you. If that's the case, what do you need with a Savior or with mercy? What need do you have for justification? If you are living this way, you are probably already tired of my book, because it will be of no interest to you. If you allow yourself to be proud in this way, listen to me for a little while longer. What you're trusting in will amount to nothing in eternity, because when your righteousness is all your own working you are either a deceiver or are deceived. You are lost, as sure as you are alive, because the Scripture cannot lie, and it says plainly, *there is not a righteous man on earth who continually does good and who never sins* (Ecclesiastes 7:20).

> I have no gospel to preach to the self-righteous.

In any case, I have no gospel to preach to the self-righteous. I say this because Jesus Christ didn't come to call the righteous, and I am not going to do what He didn't do. If I called you to accept the true gospel, and you think you're already righteous, you wouldn't come. Therefore, I won't call you for less than the moral qualities distinctive to Jesus. No, instead I tell you to look at that righteousness of yours until you see what a delusion it is. It isn't even half as substantial as a cobweb. Be done with it. Run from it!

The only people who can realize their need for justification are those who know they can't accomplish it on their own (Galatians 2:16). It is something that must be done for them, in order to make them just before the judgment seat of God (Ephesians 2:8). The Lord only does what is needful, and in His infinite wisdom, He never attempts what is unnecessary. For Him to make a person just who is already just isn't a work for God – that's a job for a fool. But to make an unjust person just – that is work for infinite love and mercy. To *justify the ungodly* – this is a miracle worthy of God.

Think of it this way. If a physician discovered a precious cure proven to work, to whom would that physician be sent? Would it be to those who are perfectly healthy? I don't think so. If he's sent to a district where there are no sick people, there's nothing for him to do. *It is not those who are healthy who need a physician, but those who are sick* (Mark 2:17). Isn't it just as clear that the great remedies of grace and redemption are for the sick of soul? These "remedies" can't be for the spiritually whole, because they would be of no use to them.

If you feel you're spiritually sick, the physician (Jesus) has come into the world for you, *for the Son of Man has come to seek and to save that which was lost* (Luke 19:10). If you are totally undone because of your sin, you are the very person aimed at in the plan of salvation. When He arranged the system of grace, the Lord of love had people just like you in mind. Suppose a man with a generous spirit decided to forgive all who were indebted to him. It makes sense that this can only apply to those really in his debt. One person owes him a thousand dollars, another owes him fifty dollars. Each one just has to have his bill marked "paid" and the liability is wiped out. But even the most generous person can't forgive debts of those who don't owe him anything. It's even out of the power of omnipotence to forgive where there is no sin because there can be no pardon if you have no sin. Pardon must be for the guilty. Forgiveness must be for the sinful. It is absurd to talk about forgiving those who don't need forgiveness, pardoning those who have never offended.

Do you think you are doomed to be lost because you are a sinner? This is in fact the reason you can be saved. Because you confess yourself to be a sinner, I encourage you to believe grace is meant for you and others like you. One of our hymn writers even dared to say:

> *A sinner is a sacred thing;*
> *The Holy Ghost hath made him so.*

It is true that Jesus came *to seek and to save that which was lost* (Luke 19:10). He died and made a real atonement for real sinners. If people are serious about what they say when they call themselves "miserable sinners," I'm overjoyed to meet with them. I'm happy to talk all night to bona fide sinners, because the inn of mercy never closes its doors on such people. Our Lord Jesus didn't die for imaginary sins. His heart's blood was spilled to wash away our deep crimson stains, which nothing else can remove. The person who is a sinner is the kind of person Jesus Christ came to make clean.

On one occasion, a preacher preached a sermon from Luke 3:9: *the axe is already laid at the root of the trees.* He delivered it in such a way that one of his hearers said to him, "One would have thought you were preaching to criminals. Your sermon ought to have been delivered in the county jail."

"Oh no," the preacher said. "If I was preaching in the

county jail, I wouldn't preach from that text. I would preach from this one: *It is a trustworthy statement, deserving full acceptance, that Christ Jesus came into the world to save sinners*" (1 Timothy 1:15). The law is for the self-righteous, to humble their pride. The gospel is for the lost, to remove their despair.

If you aren't lost, what do you want with a Savior? Should the shepherd go after those who never went astray? Why would the woman sweep her house for the bits of money that were never out of her purse? No, the medicine is for the diseased. The making alive is for the dead. The pardon is for the guilty, and deliverance is for those who are bound. The opening of eyes is for those who are blind. How can the Savior, His death upon the cross, and the gospel of forgiveness be explained, unless it is based on the belief that men are guilty and worthy of condemnation? The sinner is the gospel's reason for existence.

> The law is for the self-righteous, to humble their pride. The gospel is for the lost, to remove their despair.

My friend, as this word comes through the pages of this book, if you are undeserving or deserving of hell, you are the sort of person for whom the gospel is intended, arranged, and proclaimed. God *justifies the ungodly.*

I want to make this very clear and I hope I already have. But still, plain as it is, it is only the Lord who can make a person see it. At first, it seems most amazing that salvation could really be for a person lost and guilty. We think it must be for the one who is penitent, forgetting that repentance is a part of salvation. Such a person thinks, "I must clean up my life and do this and that." All of this is true, because his life will change in this way as the result of salvation, but salvation comes to him before he has any of the results of salvation. It comes while he deserves only this bare, beggarly, base, abominable description, *ungodly.* When God's gospel comes to justify him, that is all he is.

Therefore, I urge all who read this who recognize they have no good thing about them – who fear they haven't even got a good feeling or anything whatsoever that can speak well of them to God – to firmly believe our gracious God is able and willing to take them without anything to recommend them and to forgive them freely, not because they are good, but because He is good. Doesn't He make His sun to shine on the evil as well as on the good? Doesn't He give fruitful seasons and send the rain and the sunshine in their time upon the most ungodly nations? Even Sodom had its sun and Gomorrah had its dew.

The great grace of God surpasses anything you or I can conceive. As high as the heavens are above the earth, so high are God's thoughts above our thoughts (Isaiah 55:8-9). He can abundantly pardon. Jesus Christ came into the world to save sinners. Forgiveness is for the guilty. Don't attempt to touch up your flaws and make yourself appear to be something other than what you really are. Instead, come to Him who *justifies the ungodly* as you are.

A short time ago, a great artist painted a part of the city in which he lived. For historic purposes, he wanted to include in his picture certain characters well known in the town. An unkempt, ragged, filthy crossing sweeper was known to everybody and there was a suitable place for him in the picture. The artist said to this ragged and rugged individual, "I will pay you well if you come to my studio and let me paint your likeness." The crossing sweeper came around in the morning but was quickly sent about his business because he'd washed his face, combed his hair, and donned a respectable suit of clothes. For this piece of art, he was needed as a beggar and wasn't invited in any other capacity. In the same way, the gospel will receive you into its halls if you come as a sinner, not otherwise. Don't wait until you change your ways, but come immediately for salvation. God *justifies the ungodly* and accepts you where you are now. His justification meets you in your worst condition.

> Don't wait until you change your ways, but come immediately for salvation.

Come in your disheveled state. I mean, come to your heavenly Father in all your sin and sinfulness. Come to Jesus just as you are, leprous, filthy, naked, not fit to live or die. Come, you who are the rubbish of creation. Though you hardly dare to hope for anything but death, come to Him. Though a cloud of heavy despair hangs over you, pressing in on you like a horrible nightmare, come and ask the Lord to justify another ungodly one – you. Why wouldn't He? This great mercy of God is meant for people like you.

I put it in the language straight from the Bible because I can't put it more strongly. The Lord God

Himself takes on this gracious title, *Him who justi-fies the ungodly.* Those who by nature are ungodly, He makes just and causes to be treated as righteous. Isn't that wonderful news? Don't put this off until you've taken time to consider this matter.

# Chapter 2

# It Is God That Justifieth

What a wonderful thing it is, this being justified – pardoned and cleared from guilt. If we never broke the laws of God, we wouldn't need to be justified because we'd be just in ourselves. The person who has done the things he should all his life and has never done anything which he shouldn't is justified by the law. But I'm quite sure you're not that sort. You have too much honesty to pretend to be without sin and as a result you need to be justified. However, if you try to justify yourself, you'll simply be deceiving yourself. Therefore, don't try it. It is never worth it.

If you ask other people to justify you, what can they do? You can make some of them speak well of you for small favors, and others will speak evil of you for less. Their judgment isn't worth much.

Our text says, *God is he that justifies*, which is a lot more to the point. It's an astonishing fact, and one we ought to carefully consider. In the first place, nobody but God would ever think of justifying those who are guilty. They've lived in open rebellion and committed evil with both hands. They've gone from bad to worse and turned back to sin even after they hurt because of it and were forced to leave it for awhile. They've broken the law and trampled on the gospel. They've refused declarations of mercy and have persisted in ungodliness. How can they be forgiven and justified?

The people in their lives look at this and bleakly say, "They are hopeless cases." Even Christians look at them with sorrow rather than with hope. But that is not how their God sees them. He chose some of them before the foundation of the world, and in the splendor of His electing grace He won't rest until He has justified them and made them to be accepted in the Beloved. Isn't it written, *And these whom He predestined, He also called; and these whom He called, He also justified; and these whom He justified, He also glorified* (Romans 8:30)? When you look at it in this way, you see there are some whom the Lord agrees to justify. Why shouldn't you and I be among them?

No one but God would ever have thought of justifying me. I'm a wonder to myself and don't doubt that others view grace in others similarly. Consider Saul of Tarsus[1], who was born to Jewish parents who possessed Roman citizenship. He studied Jewish law under the famous rabbi Gamaliel and later worked against God's servants to destroy the early church. He entered homes of believers and placed them in prison. Like a hungry

---

1    Acts 9

wolf, he worried the lambs and the sheep at every turn, but God struck him down on the road to Damascus while he was on his way to arrest believers there. God changed his heart on that road, and so fully justified him that before long he became the greatest preacher of justification by faith who ever lived.

Saul of Tarsus changed his name from the Hebrew Saul to his Gentile name Paul and was sent by God to the Gentiles with the good news. He must often have marveled that he was justified by faith in Christ Jesus, because he was once a determined stickler for salvation by the works of the law. No one but God would have ever thought of justifying such a man as Saul the persecutor, but the Lord God is glorious in grace.

> All sin is against God, and if we have sinned against God, it is in God's power to forgive because the sin is against Him.

Even if someone thought about justifying the ungodly, no one but God could do it, because it is impossible for a person to forgive offenses which haven't been committed against them. Yes, you can forgive a person who has injured you in some way, and I hope you will, but no third-party person can forgive the offender apart from you. If the wrong is done to you, the pardon must come from you. However, all sin is against God, and if we have sinned against God, it is in God's power to forgive because the sin is against Him. That is why in Psalm 51:4 David says, *Against You, You only, I have sinned and done what is evil in Your sight*, for God can forgive the offense because He is the One against whom the offense is committed.

If it pleases Him, our great Creator can forgive the debt we owe to God. And if He forgives it, it is cancelled. No one but the great God whom we sinned against can blot out that sin. Therefore, let's make sure we go to Him and seek mercy at His hands and not be led astray by those who would want us to confess to them instead of to God. They have no authority in the Word of God for their claims. Even if they were appointed to declare absolution in God's name, it's still better to go directly to the great Lord through Jesus Christ, the Mediator, to seek and find pardon at His hand. It is better to see to matters of your soul yourself, rather than to leave them in some man's hands.

Only God can justify the ungodly, but He can do it to perfection. He casts our sins behind His back. He blots them out, and He says that though they are sought for, they won't be found (Isaiah 43:25). With no other reason than His own infinite goodness, He has prepared a glorious way by which He makes scarlet sins as white as snow (Isaiah 1:18), and removes our transgressions from us as far as the east is from the west (Psalm 103:12). He says, *I will remember their sins no more* (Hebrews 8:12). He does whatever is necessary to make an end of sin. One of the old prophets called out in amazement, *Who is a God like You, who pardons iniquity and passes over the rebellious act of the remnant of His possession? He does not retain His anger forever, because He delights in unchanging love* (Micah 7:18).

We're not speaking of justice now, nor are we talking about God's dealing with men according to their rewards. If you agree to deal with the righteous Lord on the law's terms, you are threatened with everlasting wrath, because according to the law, that's what you deserve. *He has not dealt with us according to our sins, nor rewarded us according to our iniquities* (Psalm 103:10), but now He treats us on terms of free grace and infinite compassion. He says, *I will heal their apostasy, I will love them freely* (Hosea 14:4).

Believe it. It is certain and true that the great God is able to treat the guilty with abundant mercy. He is able to treat the ungodly as if they've always lived godly. Read the parable of the prodigal son carefully (Luke 15:11-32), and you'll see how the forgiving father received the returning wanderer with as much love as if he'd never gone away and never contaminated himself with harlots. The mercy he showed went so far that the elder brother began to grumble about it. But the father never withdrew his love.

My dear reader, no matter how guilty you may be, if you just come to God our Father by faith in Jesus Christ, He will treat you as if you've never done wrong. Do you see what a marvelous thing it is that God would think of justifying the ungodly? What do you say?

Again, I want to make this very clear. No one other than God can do this, and He still does it. Look how the apostle Paul puts the question: *Who will bring a charge against God's elect? God is the one who justifies*

(Romans 8:33). If God has justified a person it is done completely, it is done right, it is impartially done, and it is everlastingly done.

I read a statement written in a magazine against the gospel and those who preach. It stated that Christians hold some kind of theory by which we imagine sin can be removed from people. Let's be clear. We hold no theory; we declare a fact. The greatest fact under heaven is this: that Christ, by His precious blood, actually does away with sin, and God, for Christ's sake, deals with people with divine mercy. He forgives the guilty and justifies them, not according to anything He sees in them, or foresees will be in them, but according to the riches of His mercy which lie in His own heart (Ephesians 2:7). This we have preached, do preach, and will preach as long as we live. *God is the one who justifies* (Romans 8:33), that *justifies the ungodly*. He isn't ashamed of doing it, nor are we ashamed of preaching it.

The justification which comes from God is without question. If the judge clears me, who can condemn me? If the highest court in the universe has pronounced me just, who can charge me with anything? *Who is the one who condemns? Christ Jesus is He who died, yes, rather who was raised, who is at the right hand of God, who also intercedes for us* (Romans 8:34). Justification from God is a sufficient answer to an awakened conscience. The Holy Spirit breathes peace over our entire nature, and we are no longer afraid. With this justification, we can answer all the yelling and insulting language of Satan and ungodly people. With this, we will be able to die and boldly rise again, and face the last great judgement – not guilty.

I will stand boldly on that great day:

> *For who ought to my charge shall lay?*
> *While by my Lord absolved I am.*
> *From sin's tremendous curse and blame.*
> – Zinzendorf[2]

The Lord can blot out all your sins. I'm not making a shot in the dark when I say this because God's Word says, *Any sin and blasphemy shall be forgiven people* (Matthew 12:31). Though you're steeped up to your neck in crime, with a word He can remove the pollution of sin, and say, *I am willing; be cleansed* (Matthew 8:3). The Lord is a great forgiver.

"I believe in the forgiveness of sins[3]." Do you?

He can even at this moment declare, *Your faith has saved you; go in peace* (Luke 7:50), and if He does this, no power in heaven or earth, or under the earth, can

> You couldn't forgive your fellow man if they offended you like you've offended God, but don't measure God by yourself.

place you under suspicion, much less under wrath. Don't doubt the power of almighty love. You couldn't forgive your fellow man if they offended you like you've offended God, but don't measure God by yourself. His thoughts and ways are way above yours – like the heavens are high above the earth (Isaiah 55:8-9).

You might say, "It would be a huge miracle if the

---

2    Charles B. Snepp, ed., *Songs of Grace and Glory for Private, Family, and Public Worship* (London: W. Hunt & Co., 1872).

3    The Apostles' Creed.

Lord were to pardon me." You're right. It would be an absolute miracle, and so He is likely to do it, because He does *great and mighty things, which you do not know* (Jeremiah 33:3).

In my own case, I was stuck with such a horrible sense of guilt that it made my life miserable. But when I heard the command, *Turn to Me and be saved, all the ends of the earth; For I am God, and there is no other* (Isaiah 45:22), I looked to Him and in a moment the Lord justified me. As I looked to Him, I saw Jesus Christ made sin for me and that sight gave me rest (Matthew 11:28).

When those who were bitten by the fiery serpents in the wilderness looked to the serpent of brass they were healed immediately (Numbers 21:9). This is how it was when I looked to the crucified Savior. The Holy Spirit, who enabled me to believe, gave me peace through believing. Before this, I felt condemned, but once I believed, I knew without a doubt I was forgiven, because the Word of God declared it. I had felt my condemnation was certain, and my conscience agreed. But when the Lord justified me, I was just as sure by the same proof. The Word of the Lord in the Scripture says, *He who believes in Him is not judged* (John 3:18), and my conscience bears witness that I believed and that God in pardoning me is just. As a result, I have the witness of the Holy Spirit and my own conscience, and these two agree (Romans 9:1). Oh, how I wish you would receive God's declaration

> The Holy Spirit, who enabled me to believe, gave me peace through believing.

on this matter, and you would immediately have the witness in yourself also.

I dare to say that a sinner justified by God stands on more certain footing than a righteous man justified by his works, if there could be such a person. For we can never be sure of whether we've done enough works, and our conscience would always be uneasy wondering if we may have come up short. We only have the shaky verdict of human judgment to rely on, but when God justifies and the Holy Spirit bears witness – that gives us peace with God. This is why we can feel the matter is sure and settled, and we *enter that rest* (Hebrews 4:3). No tongue can explain the depth of that calm which comes over the soul that receives the peace of God which passes all understanding (Philippians 4:7).

Chapter 3

# The Just and the Justifier

W e have seen the ungodly justified and have
considered the great truth that only God can
justify any person. Now we will take it a step further and
ask, how can a just God justify guilty people? We can
find the answer in the words of Paul in Romans 3:21b-26:
*the righteousness of God has been manifested, being
witnessed by the Law and the Prophets, even the righteousness of God through faith in Jesus Christ for all
those who believe; for there is no distinction; for all have
sinned and fall short of the glory of God, being justified
as a gift by His grace through the redemption which is
in Christ Jesus; whom God displayed publicly as a propitiation in His blood through faith. This was to dem-
onstrate His righteousness, because in the forbearance
of God He passed over the sins previously committed;
for the demonstration, I say, of His righteousness at the*

*present time, so that He would be just and the justifier of the one who has faith in Jesus.*

Now, if you'll permit me, I want to share a bit of my personal experience with you. While under the hand of the Holy Spirit, I was convicted of sin. I had a clear and sharp sense of the justice of God. Sin, whatever it might be to other people, became an intolerable burden to me. It wasn't so much that I feared hell, but that I feared sin. I knew I was horribly guilty and felt that if God didn't punish me for sin, He ought to condemn such sin as mine.

I sat on the judgment seat, and I condemned myself to death. I admitted that if I were God, I could do nothing other than send such a guilty creature as me to the lowest hell. While going through this, I also had a deep concern for the honor of God's name and the integrity of His moral leadership on my mind. It didn't set right with my conscience that I could be forgiven unjustly. The sin I committed had to be punished. I struggled with the question of how God could be just, and yet justify me – the guilty. In my heart, I asked, "How can He be just and yet the justifier?" I was worried and wearied with this question and couldn't see any answer to it. Certainly, I could never have invented an answer that would satisfy my conscience.

To my way of thinking, the doctrine of the atonement is one of the surest proofs of the divine inspiration of Holy Scripture. For my readers who don't know

> I admitted that if I were God, I could do nothing other than send such a guilty creature as me to the lowest hell.

what the doctrine of atonement is, it is that Christ Jesus died on the cross for our sins (1 Corinthians 15:3). In this way, He fulfilled the sacrificial system of the old covenant and restored our relationship with God and changed our lives forever. Who would or could have thought of the just Ruler dying for the unjust rebel? This isn't a teaching of human mythology or a fantasy of poetical imagination. This act of atoning for a crime – of making satisfaction for an offense by which the guilt is done away and the obligation of the offended person to be punished for the crime is canceled – is only known about because it is a fact. Fiction could never have conceived it, for God Himself ordained it.

I had heard the plan of salvation by the sacrifice of Jesus from the time I was a youth, but in my innermost soul I didn't understand or know any more about it than if I had been born and bred a savage unbelieving man. The light of the truth was there in Scripture, but I was blind. I needed the Lord to make the matter clear to me. When He did, it came to me like a new revelation, as fresh as if I'd never read about Jesus being declared the propitiation or atonement for sins so God can be just.

Every newborn child of God receives such a revelation – that glorious doctrine of the substitution of the Lord Jesus. I came to understand salvation was possible through substitutional sacrifice and that provision for such a substitution had been made in the Son of God – the co-equal and co-eternal with the Father. He had been made the promised Head of a chosen people from the beginning so He could suffer for them and save them. Considering that our fall from God's ways wasn't a personal one in the beginning, because sin began with our ancestral representative, the first Adam, we understand that by a second representative, Jesus, it became possible for us to be recovered – saved from sin – because He agreed to be the covenant Head of His people, to be their second Adam. *So also it is written, The first man, Adam, became a living soul. The last Adam became a life-giving spirit* (1 Corinthians 15:45).

I saw that before I actually sinned I had a fallen, spiritually dead nature through my first father's sin, and I rejoiced that it became possible – based on the facts and evidence of Scripture – for me to come to life through a second Head and representative. The fall by Adam left a loophole of escape. Another Adam – *the last Adam* – can undo the ruin caused by the first. While I was anxious about the possibility of a just God pardoning me for my sin, I understood and saw by faith that this last Adam is Jesus, the Son of God who became man. In His blessed body, He bore my sin on the cross. The punishment I deserved because *the wages of sin is death* (Romans 6:23) was laid on Him. I was healed through His affliction because *the free gift of God is eternal life in Christ Jesus our Lord* (Romans 6:23).

That's what God showed me. Have you ever seen that? Have you ever understood how God can be completely just, not cancel or diminish the penalty, but be infinitely merciful and still able to *justify the ungodly* who turn to Him? It's possible because the Son of God, supremely glorious in His matchless person, vindicated me by fulfilling the law by bearing the sentence due me. Therefore, God is able to pass by my sin. The law of God was upheld more by the death of Christ than if all sinners were sent to hell. For the Son of God to suffer for sin was a more glorious establishment of the authority of God than for the whole human race to suffer.

Jesus endured the death penalty on our behalf. Do you see the wonder in this? See Him hanging on the cross! If you can see it, you see the most significant sight you'll ever see. The Son of God and Son of Man hanging there in one person bearing unspeakable pain – *the just for the unjust* – to bring us to God (1 Peter 3:18).

Oh, the glory of that sight. The innocent punished. The Holy One condemned. The ever-blessed made a curse. The infinitely glorious put to a shameful death in my place, in your place. The more I look at the sufferings **Jesus endured the death penalty on our behalf.** of the Son of God the more certain I am that they meet my case. Why did He suffer, if not to turn aside the penalty of sin from us? So if He turned it aside by His death, then it is out of the way. Those who believe in Him no longer need to fear it, because since atonement is made, God is able to forgive without shaking the foundation of His throne or tarnishing the law in the least. The tremendous question put forth by our conscience is satisfied.

The wrath of God against sin is more terrible than we can comprehend, whatever our sin may be. Moses said it very well, *Who understands the power of Your anger?* (Psalm 90:11). Yet when we hear the Lord of glory cry, *Why have you forsaken me?* (Matthew 27:46) and see Him yielding up the spirit, we feel the justice

27

of God abundantly vindicated by the obedience of such a perfect and terrible death given by such a divine person. If God Himself bows before His own law, what more can be done? There is more in the atonement as a method of merit, than there is in all human sin to deserve blame or punishment.

The great gulf of Jesus' loving self-sacrifice can swallow up the mountains of our sins – all of them. For the sake of the infinite good of this one representative Man, the Lord may well look with favor upon other people, however unworthy they may be. It's a miracle of miracles that the Lord Jesus Christ would stand in our stead and that "He bore, that we might never bear, Th'Almighty's righteous ire."[4]

> If you believe in Jesus (that is the point), then your sins were carried away by Him.

But He has done so. *It is finished* (John 19:30). God will spare the sinner because He didn't spare His Son. God can pass over your sins because He laid those sins on His only begotten Son nearly two thousand years ago. If you believe in Jesus (that is the point), then your sins were carried away by Him as the scapegoat for His people.

What is it to believe in Him? It's more than saying, "He is God and the Savior." It means we must trust Him wholly and entirely. You must accept Him for all your salvation from this time forward and forever as your Lord, your Master, your all. If you will accept Jesus, He has accepted you already. If you believe on Him, you

---

4    John Nelson Darby, ed., *Hymns for the Little Flock* (Oak Park, IL: Bible Truth Publishers, 1881), Section 3.

cannot go to hell, because that would make the sacrifice of Christ of no effect. It can't be that a sacrifice would be accepted and then the soul for whom that sacrifice has been received still dies.

If the believing soul could still be condemned, then why a sacrifice? If Jesus died in my place, why should I also die? Every believer can claim that the sacrifice was actually made for him. He's laid hold of it by faith and made it his own. As a result, he can know for certain that he can never perish. The Lord wouldn't receive this offering on our behalf and then condemn us to die. The Lord can't read our pardon written in the blood of His Son and then cut us down. That would be impossible. I pray you will accept the grace offered to you immediately and look to Jesus to begin at the beginning – to the source of mercy to guilty man – Jesus.

He *justifies the ungodly. God is he that justifies them*, and for that reason it can only be accomplished through the atoning sacrifice of His divine Son. Consequently, it can be justly done – so justly done that no one will ever question it. So thoroughly done that in the last day, when heaven and earth pass away, there will be no one who will deny the validity of the justification. *Who is the one who condemns? Christ Jesus is He who died, yes, rather who was raised, who is at the right hand of God, who also intercedes for us* (Romans 8:34).

Will you come into this lifeboat, just as you are? It offers safety from the wreck. Accept the undisputable deliverance. You say, "I have nothing with me," but you aren't asked to bring anything with you. People who escape for their lives will leave even their clothes behind. Leap for salvation just as you are.

I tell you this about myself to encourage you. My sole hope for going to heaven lies in the full atonement made on Calvary's cross for the ungodly. I rely firmly on that. I don't have a shadow of hope anywhere else. You are in the same condition. Neither of us has anything of our own worth a bit of trust. Let's join hands and stand together at the foot of the cross, and trust our souls immediately and completely to Him who shed His blood for the guilty. We will be saved by one and the same Savior. What more can I do to prove my own confidence in the gospel which I set before you?

# Chapter 4

# Concerning Deliverance from Sinning

At this point, I want to speak clearly to those who understand God's method of justification by faith in Christ Jesus, but who still struggle with sin in their lives. We can never be happy, restful, or spiritually healthy until we become holy. To be holy, we must be rid of sin, but how can we accomplish this impossible task?

This is the life-or-death question of many people. The old nature is very strong, and you may have tried to curb and tame it only to find it won't be subdued. You're anxious to do better but only end up doing worse. The heart is so hard, the will is so obstinate, the passions so furious, the thoughts so volatile, the imagination so out of control, and the desires so wild, that you feel like you have a den of wild beasts within you, which will eat you up rather than be ruled by the Lord.

We can say of our fallen nature what the Lord said to Job concerning the large sea monster Leviathan: *Will you play with him as with a bird, or will you bind him for your maidens?* (Job 41:5). A man might as well hope to hold the north wind in the hollow of his hand as to expect to control those unruly powers which lie within his fallen nature by his own strength. This is a greater feat than anything done by the strength of the fabled Hercules. For this, God is needed.

One might say, "I believe Jesus will forgive sin, but my trouble is that I sin again. Within me, I feel such awful tendencies to do evil. As surely as a stone flung into the air quickly falls to the ground again, so am I with sin. For though I'm sent up to heaven by sincere preaching, I return again to my hard-hearted state. Sadly, I'm easily fascinated with sin. It's like I'm held under a spell where I can't escape from my own foolishness."

> We want to be purified as well as pardoned.

If this is your struggle, take heart. Salvation would be sadly incomplete if it didn't deal with this part of our ruined condition. We want to be purified as well as pardoned. Justification (being made righteous) without sanctification (becoming holy) would not be salvation at all. It would be like calling a leper clean and leaving him to die of his disease. It would forgive the rebellion and allow the rebel to remain an enemy to his king. It would remove the consequences but overlook the cause, and this would leave us with an endless and hopeless task. It would stop the stream of sin for a time, but leave an open fountain of defilement, which would sooner or later burst forth with increased power.

Remember that the Lord Jesus came to take away sin in three ways. He came to remove the penalty of sin, the power of sin, and the presence of sin. You can reach the second part immediately. The power of sin can be broken at once, and then you'll be on the road to the third part – the removal of the presence of sin. We *know that He appeared in order to take away sins* (1 John 3:5).

The angel said of our Lord, *you shall call His name Jesus, for He will save His people from their sins* (Matthew 1:21). Our Lord Jesus came to destroy in us the works of the Devil. The same thing stated at our Lord's birth was also declared in His death. When the soldier pierced His side, a flow of blood and water came out, which clarified the double cure by which we are delivered from the guilt and the defilement of sin.

However, if you're troubled about the power of sin in your life and the tendencies of your nature, as you may well be, here is a promise for you. Have faith in this promise, because it is founded in that covenant of grace which is sure. God, who cannot lie, has said, *I will give you a new heart and put a new spirit within you; and I will remove the heart of stone from your flesh and give you a heart of flesh* (Ezekiel 36:26).

You see, it is all *I will*, and *I put*. *I will give* and *I will remove*. This is the royal style of the King of Kings, who is able to accomplish His will. No word of His will ever fall to the ground (1 Samuel 3:19).

The Lord knows very well that you can't change

your own heart, and you can't cleanse your own nature. But He also knows He can do both. He can cause the Ethiopian to change his skin, and the leopard his spots. Hear this and be amazed: He can create you a second time. He can cause you to be born again. This is a miracle of grace, and the Holy Spirit will perform it. It would be a miraculous thing if a person could stand at the foot of Niagara Falls and say something that would cause the river Niagara to begin to run upstream and send that torrent of water leaping back up that great precipice over which it now rolls in stupendous force. Nothing but the power of God could achieve such a marvel.

This Niagara Falls example offers a fitting parallel to what takes place if the course of your nature is totally reversed. All things are possible with God. He can reverse the direction of your desires and the current of your life. Instead of going downward – away from God – He can make your whole being have a tendency to flow upward toward God. In fact, that is what the Lord has promised to do for all who are in the covenant. We know from Scripture that all believers are in the covenant. Let me share the words again: *And I will give them one heart, and put a new spirit within them. And I will take the heart of stone out of their flesh and give them a heart of flesh* (Ezekiel 11:19).

What a wonderful promise. Christ Jesus agrees with it, and we can say "amen" to the glory of God. Let's lay hold of it, accept it as true, and adopt it for ourselves. Then it will be fulfilled in us, and in days and years to come, we'll be able to sing of that wondrous change which the sovereign grace of God has worked in us.

Consider this. When the Lord takes away the stony heart, that deed is done. Once that is done, no known power can ever take away the new heart He gives and the right spirit which He puts within us. *For the gifts and the calling of God are irrevocable* (Romans 11:29). This *irrevocable* is on His part. He will not change His mind. He doesn't take away what He has already given. Let Him renew you, and you will be renewed. People's resolutions to change and their efforts to clean up their lives soon come to an end, for *like a dog that returns to its vomit is a fool who repeats his folly* (Proverbs 26:11). But when God puts a new heart into us, it is a new heart to the fullest extent.

> Let Him renew you, and you will be renewed.

To put it simply, have you ever heard of Mr. Rowland Hill's illustration of the cat and the sow? I will offer my own version to illustrate our Savior's significant word, *Unless one is born again he cannot see the kingdom of God* (John 3:3).

Do you see that cat? What a clean creature she is. How cleverly she washes herself with her tongue and her paws. It is quite an appealing sight. Did you ever see a sow do that? No, you never did. It is contrary to its nature. It prefers to wallow in the mire. Go and teach a sow to wash itself, and see how little success you achieve. It would be a big sanitary improvement if swine would be clean, but teaching them to wash and clean themselves like the cat would be a useless task.

You can wash that sow by force, but it will just hurry back to the mire and become as foul as ever. The only way you can get a sow to wash itself is to transform it into a cat. Then it will wash and be clean, but not until then. Suppose that transformation is accomplished, then what was difficult or impossible is easy enough. From that time forward the swine will be fit for your parlor and the rug in front of your hearth.

It is the same with an ungodly person. You can't force them to do what a renewed man does willingly. You can teach them and set a good example for them, but they can't learn the art of holiness, because they don't have a mind to do it. Their nature leads them another way. When the Lord makes a new creation of them, then everything is different. This change is so great, that I once heard a convert say, "Either all the world is changed, or else I am." The new nature follows after right as naturally as the old nature wanders after wrong. What a blessing to receive such a nature. Only the Holy Spirit can give it.

Did it ever strike you what a wonderful thing it is for the Lord to give a new heart and a right spirit to a person? Perhaps you've seen a lobster which has fought with another lobster and lost one of its claws, and a new claw has grown. That is a remarkable thing, but it's much more astounding that a person could have a new heart given to him. This is a miracle beyond the powers of nature.

There is a tree that when you cut off one of its limbs, another one can grow in its place. But can you change the tree? Can you sweeten sour sap? Can you make the thorn tree bear figs? No, but you can graft something better into it. This is the analogy nature gives us of the work of grace, but to absolutely change the vital sap of the tree would really be a miracle. It is just such a wonder and mystery that the power of God works in all who believe in Jesus.

If you yield yourself to His divine working, the Lord will alter your nature. He will subdue the old nature and breathe new life into you. Put your trust in the Lord Jesus Christ, and He will take the stony heart out of your flesh and give you a tender heart of flesh. Where everything was hard, everything will become tender. Where everything was vicious, everything will become virtuous. Where everything tended to go downward, everything will rise upward with spontaneous force. The lion of anger will give way to the lamb of meekness, and the raven of uncleanness will flee before the dove of purity. The vile serpent of deceit will be trodden under the heel of truth.

> Thieves are made honest, drunkards sober, liars truthful, and scoffers zealous.

With my own eyes, I've seen such marvelous changes of moral and spiritual character that I know there's no one who is hopeless. If it were fitting, I could point out women who were once unchaste but are now pure as the driven snow. And I could do the same with men who were once blasphemers who now delight those around them by their intense devotion to Christ. Thieves are made honest, drunkards sober, liars truthful, and scoffers zealous. *For the grace of God has appeared, bringing salvation to all men, instructing us to deny ungodliness and worldly desires and to live sensibly, righteously and godly in the present age;* and, dear reader, it will do the same for you (Titus 2:11-12).

You say, "I can't make this change." Who said you could? The Scripture which we have quoted isn't talking about what man will do, but about what God will do. It is God's promise, and it is for Him to fulfill. Trust in Him to fulfill His Word to you, and it will be done.

"But how is it to be accomplished?" you ask.

What business is that of yours? Must the Lord explain His methods before you will believe Him? The Lord's working in this matter is a great mystery. The Holy Spirit performs it and it is a spiritual matter, not a physical matter. He who made the promise has the responsibility of keeping the promise, and He is equal to the occasion. God who promises this marvelous change will surely carry it out in as many as receive Him, for *to them He gave the right to become children of God, even to those who believe in His name* (John 1:12).

How I pray you would believe – that you would do the gracious Lord the justice to believe that He can and will do this great miracle for you. I pray you would believe that God cannot lie. Trust Him for a new heart and a right spirit, for He can give them to you. May the Lord give you faith in His promise, faith in His Son, faith in the Holy Spirit, and faith in Him, and to Him shall be praise and honor and glory forever and ever! Amen.

# Chapter 5

# By Grace Through Faith

I think it is best to turn to the side for a moment to ask my reader to adoringly observe the fountainhead – the source of our salvation, which is the grace of God. *By grace you have been saved.* Because God is gracious, sinful men are forgiven, converted, purified, and saved. It isn't because of anything in them or that ever can be in them, or anything they've done or ever can do that they are saved. It is because of the boundless love, goodness, pity, compassion, mercy, and grace of God. Linger a moment at the wellhead. Behold the pure river of the water of life as it proceeds out of the throne of God and of the Lamb.

> *For by grace you have been saved through faith.* (Ephesians 2:8)

Who can measure the extensiveness of the grace of God? Who can fathom its depth? Like all the rest of the divine attributes, His grace is infinite. God is full of love, because God is love (1 John 4:8). God is full of goodness. The very name "God" is short for "good." Limitless goodness and love enter into the very heart of the Godhead, because *His lovingkindness is everlasting* (Psalm 136:1). People are not destroyed because His compassions never fail (Lamentations 3:22), but instead, sinners are brought to Him and forgiven.

Remember this, or you may make the mistake of fixing your mind so much on faith, which is the channel of salvation, that you forget the grace which is the fountain and source even of faith itself. Faith is the work of God's grace in us. No one can say that Jesus is the Christ but by the Holy Spirit (1 Corinthians 12:3). "Christ hath also said: 'No man cometh unto Me, except the Father, which hath sent Me, draw him.'"[5] So that faith which results in coming to Christ is the consequence of divine drawing which pulls us toward the Father. Grace is the first and last moving cause of salvation, and faith, essential as it is, is only an important part of the machinery which grace employs. We are saved *through faith*, but salvation is *by grace*. Let those words sound out as if announced with the archangel's trumpet: *By grace you have been saved*. What happy news this is for the undeserving.

Faith works like a channel or conduit pipe while grace is the fountain and the stream. Faith is the aqueduct along which the flood of mercy flows to refresh the thirsty sons of men. It is a great pity when the aqueduct is broken. It is a sad sight to see the many

---

5    Martin Luther, *The Theologia Germanica of Martin Luther* (1516).

noble aqueducts around Rome which no longer carry water into the city, because arches are broken and the marvelous structures are in ruins. The aqueduct must be kept whole and intact to carry the flow, and, even then, faith must be founded in truth and be firm, leading right up to God and coming right down to us, so it can become a functional channel of mercy to our souls.

Again, I remind you that faith is only the channel or aqueduct and not the original source of blessing. We must not look to faith in a way that elevates it above the grace of God, which is the divine source of all blessing. Don't think of faith as if it is the independent source of your salvation. Our new life is found *fixing our eyes on Jesus* (Hebrews 12:2), not in looking to our own faith. By faith all things become possible to us, yet the power isn't in the faith, but in the God upon whom faith relies. Grace is the powerful engine and faith is the chain by which the coach of the soul is attached. The righteousness of faith isn't the moral excellence of faith, but rather the righteousness of Jesus Christ which faith grasps and seizes hold of. Peace within the soul isn't derived from the contemplation of our own faith. It comes to us from Him who is our peace, the hem of whose garment faith touches and virtue comes out of into the soul.

See then that the weakness of your faith won't destroy you. A trembling hand can still receive a golden gift. The Lord's salvation can come to us even if we have faith the

> By faith all things become possible to us, yet the power isn't in the faith, but in the God upon whom faith relies.

size of a grain of a mustard seed. The power lies in the grace of God and not in our faith. Great messages can be sent along slender wires, and the peace-giving witness of the Holy Spirit can reach the heart by means of a thread-like faith which seems almost unable to sustain its own weight. Think more about Him to whom you look than about the look itself. See nothing but Jesus, and the grace of God revealed in Him.

Chapter 6

# Faith – What Is It?

What is this faith we read about in Ephesians 2:8 which says, *by grace you have been saved through faith*? Faith has many descriptions, but almost all the definitions I've come across have made me understand it less than I did before I saw them. We can explain faith until nobody understands it. I hope I won't be guilty of that, because faith is simple. But perhaps because of its simplicity, it is more difficult to explain.

What is faith? It is made up of three things: knowledge, belief, and trust. Knowledge comes first. *How will they believe in Him whom they have not heard?* (Romans 10:14). I want to be informed about a fact before I believe it. *Faith comes from hearing* (Romans 10:17). We must first hear, so we can know what is to be believed. *And those who know Your name will put their trust in You* (Psalm 9:10). A degree of knowledge is essential to faith. For this reason, getting the knowledge is important. *Incline your ear and come to Me. Listen, that you may live* (Isaiah 55:3). Such was the word of Isaiah the prophet, and it's still the word of the gospel. Search the Scriptures and learn what the Holy Spirit teaches concerning Christ and His salvation. Seek to know God. *For he who comes to God must believe that He is and that He is a rewarder of those who seek Him* (Hebrews 11:6). May the Holy Spirit give you the spirit of knowledge and of the fear of the Lord. Know the gospel:

**Know the gospel, know what the good news is.**

know what the good news is, how it talks of free forgiveness and about a change of heart, of adoption into the family of God, and about countless other blessings.

Specifically, know Christ Jesus the Son of God, the Savior who is united to us by His human nature, and who is still one with God. Because of this, He is able to act as the Mediator between God and man – able to lay His hand on both to be the connecting link between the sinner and the judge of all the earth. Endeavor to know more and more about Christ Jesus. Above all, endeavor to know the doctrine of the sacrifice of Christ, because the point on which saving faith mainly fixes itself is this: *God was in Christ reconciling the world to Himself, not counting their trespasses against them* (2 Corinthians 5:19). Know that Jesus had *become a curse for us-for it is written, Cursed is everyone who hangs on a tree* (Galatians 3:13). Drink deeply of the doctrine of the substitutionary work of Christ, because the sweetest possible comfort to the guilty is found in it, since the Lord *has made Him who knew no sin to be sin on our behalf, so that we might become the righteousness of God in Him* (2 Corinthians 5:21). Faith begins with knowledge.

Based on this knowledge, the mind goes on to believe these things are true. The soul believes God hears the cries of a sincere heart, that the gospel is from God, and that justification by faith is the great truth which God has revealed in these last days by His Spirit. Along with the mind and the soul, the heart believes Jesus is, in fact and in truth, our God and Savior, the Redeemer of mankind, the prophet, priest, and King of His people. All this is accepted as certain and unquestionable truth.

I pray you can immediately come to accept this truth and firmly believe that *the blood of Jesus His Son cleanses us from all sin* (1 John 1:7), and that His sacrifice is complete and fully accepted by God on our behalf, so that *he who believes in Him is not judged* (John 3:18). Believe these truths, because the difference between common faith and saving faith lies mainly in the subjects which exercise it. Believe the witness of God just like you would believe the testimony of your own father or friend. *If we receive the testimony of men, the testimony of God is greater* (1 John 5:9).

So far, you've made progress toward faith, but you still need one more ingredient to complete it – trust. Commit yourself to the merciful God. Place your hope in the gracious gospel. Trust your soul to the dying and living Savior and wash away your sins in the atoning blood. Accept His perfect righteousness and all is well. Trust is the lifeblood of faith. Without it, there's no saving faith.

The Puritans explained faith with the word *recumbency*. It meant "leaning on a thing." When it comes to trust, lean all your weight on Christ. An even better illustration would be to fall full length and lie on the Rock of Ages. Cast yourself on Jesus. Rest in Him. Commit yourself to Him. When you've done that, you've exercised saving faith.

Faith is not a blind thing, because faith begins with knowledge. It isn't a speculative thing, because faith believes facts of which it is sure. It isn't an unpractical, dreamy thing, because faith trusts, and stakes its destiny on the truth of revelation.

This is one way of describing what faith is. Here's another. Faith is believing Christ is what He said He is and that He will do what He promised to do, and then to expect this of Him. The Scriptures speak of Jesus Christ as being God – God in human flesh. They speak of Him as being perfect in character, made a sin offering on our behalf, and bearing our sins in His own body on the cross. The Scripture speaks of Him as having finished transgression, making an end of sin, and bringing in everlasting righteousness (Daniel 9:24).

The sacred Word also tells us that He *died and rose again* (1 Thessalonians 4:14), that He ever lives to make intercession for us (Hebrews 7:25), that He has gone up into glory, and that He has taken possession of heaven on behalf of His people. It also says that He will come again shortly and *will judge the world in righteousness; He will execute judgment for the peoples with equity* (Psalm 9:8). We must strongly believe that this is true, because the testimony of God the Father says, *This is*

*My Son, My Chosen One; listen to Him* (Luke 9:35). This is also testified by God the Holy Spirit, for the Spirit has borne witness to Christ in the inspired Word, by various miracles and by His working in the hearts of men. We are to believe this testimony to be true.

Faith also believes that Christ will do what He has promised. Since He promised that *the one who comes to Me I will certainly not cast out* (John 6:37), it is certain that He won't cast us out if we come to Him. Faith believes that since Jesus said, *The water that I will give him will become in him a well of water springing up to eternal life* (John 4:14), it must be true. And if we get this living water from Christ, it will abide in us and will well up within us in streams of holy life. Whatever Christ has promised to do He will do. We must believe this – we must look for pardon, justification, preservation, and eternal glory from His hands, according to what He has promised to believers in Him.

> If we get this living water from Christ, it will abide in us and will well up within us in streams of holy life.

For the next necessary step let us look at the fact that Jesus is what He said He is, Jesus will do what He says He will do, and for this reason we must individually trust Him, saying, "He will be to me what He says He is, and He will do for me what He has promised to do. I leave myself in the hands of Him who is appointed to save – that He can save me. I rest on His promise that He will do everything He has said." This is saving faith, and *He who believes in the Son has eternal life* (John 3:36).

No matter what dangers and difficulties you face, whatever darkness and depression, whatever weaknesses and sins – he who believes in Christ Jesus in this way *does not come into judgment, but has passed out of death into life* (John 5:24). I trust these truths can be used by the Spirit of God to direct you into immediate peace. *Do not be afraid any longer, only believe* (Mark 5:36). Trust and be at rest.

My fear is that you might rest content with an understanding of what is to be done but still never do it. The poorest real faith that's actually at work is better than the best ideal faith left floundering with speculation (James 1:22). The important thing is that we believe on the Lord Jesus right now. Never mind differences and definitions. A hungry man eats even though he doesn't understand the composition of his food, the anatomy of his mouth, or the process of digestion. He lives because he eats.

Another far more clever person can thoroughly understand the science of nutrition, but if he doesn't eat, he will die along with all his knowledge. No doubt, there are many in hell at this time who understood the doctrine of faith but didn't believe. On the other hand, not a single person who has trusted in the Lord Jesus has ever been cast out, even though he might never have been able to intelligently define his faith. Receive the Lord Jesus into your soul, and you will live forever with Him in heaven. *He who believes in the Son has eternal life* (John 3:36).

# Chapter 7

# How Can Faith Be Illustrated?

To make the matter of faith clearer still, in this chapter I'll give you a few illustrations. While only the Holy Spirit can make you see, it's my duty and joy to furnish all the light I can and to pray the divine Lord opens blind eyes. I hope you will pray the same prayer for yourself.

Faith which saves has similarities with the human frame.

It is the eye which gives vision. Via the eye, we bring into the mind things which are far away. With a glance of our eyes, we can bring the sun and faraway stars into the mind. In the same way, by trust, we bring the Lord Jesus near to us. Even though He is far away in heaven, He enters into our heart. Only look to Jesus. This message captured in the hymn "There Is Life for a Look at the Crucified One" is exactly true:

*There is life for a look at the Crucified One,*
*There is life at this moment for thee.*

Faith is like the hand which grasps. When our hand takes hold of anything, it does precisely what faith does when it appropriates Christ and the blessings of His redemption. Faith says, "Jesus is mine." Faith hears of the pardoning blood and cries, "I accept it to pardon me." Faith calls the legacies of the dying Jesus her own, and they are because faith is Christ's heir. He has given Himself and all that He has to faith. Accept what grace has provided for you. You won't be a thief, because you have a divine permit. *Let the one who wishes take the water of life without cost* (Revelation 22:17). The one who can make a treasure his own simply by grasping it will be foolish if he remains poor.

**Before food can nourish us, it must be received into us.**

Faith is like the mouth. It feeds on Christ. Before food can nourish us, it must be received into us. This is a simple matter – this eating and drinking. We willingly receive food into the mouth and it passes into our inward parts where it is absorbed. The apostle Paul says, *The word is near you, in your mouth* (Romans 10:8). To permit it to go down into the soul, all that needs to be done is to swallow it. People who are hungry and see food in front of them don't need to be taught how to eat. One would say, "Give me a knife and a fork and a chance," and would be fully prepared to do the rest.

Truly, a heart which hungers and thirsts after Christ has only to know that He is freely given, and that heart will immediately receive Him. If you are in this situation, don't hesitate to receive Jesus. You can be sure that you'll never be blamed for doing so, because *as many as received Him, to them He gave the right to become children of God* (John 1:12). He never rejects those who receive Him but rather authorizes all who come to remain sons forever.

The pursuits of life illustrate faith in many ways. The farmer buries good seed in the earth, and expects it not only to live but also to multiply. He has faith in the promise that *seedtime and harvest . . . shall not cease* (Genesis 8:22), and he is rewarded for his faith.

A merchant places his money in the care of a banker and totally trusts the honesty and soundness of the bank. He entrusts his capital into another's hands and feels far more at ease than if he had the solid gold locked up in an iron safe.

The sailor trusts himself to the sea. When he boards his ship he takes his foot from the dry land and rests it on the buoyant ocean. This couldn't be accomplished if he didn't completely cast himself upon the water.

The goldsmith puts precious metal into the fire, which seems eager to consume it, but he receives it back again from the furnace, purified by the heat.

There's nowhere you can turn in life without seeing faith in operation between one person and another or between a person and natural law. Now, just like we trust in daily life, in the same way we are to trust in God as He is revealed in Christ Jesus. Faith exists in different people in various degrees, according to the amount of their knowledge or growth in grace. Sometimes faith is little more than a simple clinging to Christ – a sense of dependence and a willingness to depend.

When you visit the seaside you'll see marine mollusks sticking to the rock. You step softly up to the rock and strike a rapid blow to the mollusk with your walking stick and off it comes. Try doing the same to the next mollusk. You've given him a warning – he heard the first blow which struck his neighbor, so he clings with all his might. You'll never get him off. You can strike and strike again and even break the rock, but our little friend, the mollusk, even though it doesn't know or understand much – it clings. This little creature isn't acquainted with the geological formation of the rock, but yet it clings. It can cling and has found something to cling to. This is the sum of all its knowledge, and it uses it for its security and salvation.

It is the mollusk's life to cling to the rock, and it's the sinner's life to cling to Jesus. Thousands of God's people have no more faith than this. They know enough to cling to Jesus with all their heart and soul, and this is sufficient for peace and eternal safety. To them, Jesus Christ is Savior strong and mighty, a Rock immovable and unchangeable. They cling to Him for dear life, and this clinging saves them. I ask you, can't you cling? Do so at once.

Faith is seen when one person relies on another because they recognize their superior knowledge. This is a higher faith than the clinging mollusk shows, because this faith knows the reason for its dependence and acts upon it. I don't think the mollusk knows much about the rock, but as faith grows, it becomes more and more intelligent. A blind man trusts himself with his guide, because he knows that his guide can see, so he trusts to walk where his guide leads him. If the poor man is born blind, he doesn't know what sight is, but he knows there is such a thing and that his guide possesses it. For this reason, he freely puts his hand into the hand of the seeing one and follows his leadership. *For we walk by faith, not by sight* (2 Corinthians 5:7).

*Blessed are they who did not see, and yet believed* (John 20:29). This is as good an example of faith as there can be. We know that Jesus has merit, power, and blessing, which we don't have, and for that reason, we gladly trust ourselves to Him to be for us what we cannot be for ourselves. We trust Him as the blind man trusts his guide. He never betrays our confidence, but He *became to us wisdom from God, and righteousness and sanctification, and redemption* (1 Corinthians 1:30).

> We know that Jesus has merit, power, and blessing, which we don't have, and for that reason, we gladly trust ourselves to Him.

Every boy that goes to school has to exert faith while learning. His teacher instructs him in geography and teaches him about the earth and the existence of certain great cities and empires. The boy doesn't know these things are true except that he believes his teacher and his books. That's what you'll have to do with Christ, if you are to be saved. You must simply know because in the Bible He tells you; believe because He assures you it is so, and trust yourself with Him because He promises salvation will be the result.

Almost everything you and I know has come to us through faith. When a scientific discovery is made and we are sure of it, on what grounds do we believe it? On the authority of certain well-known experts, whose reputations are established. We have never performed or seen their experiments, but we believe their proof. You must do the same with regard to Jesus. He teaches you certain truths and you are to be His disciple and believe His words. Because He has performed certain acts, you are to be His follower and entrust yourself to Him. He is infinitely superior to you and introduces Himself to your confidence as your Master and Lord. If you receive Him and His words, you will be saved.

Another and even higher form of faith is that faith which grows out of love. Why does a boy trust his father? The child trusts his father because he loves him. Those who have a sweet faith in Jesus, intertwined with deep affection for Him are both blessed and happy because this is a peaceful confidence. These lovers of Jesus are delighted with His character and mission. They are carried away by the loving-kindness He has shown and can't help trusting Him, because they admire, revere, and love Him so much.

The way of loving trust in the Savior can be illustrated like this. A lady is the wife of the most eminent physician of the day. Seized with a dangerous illness, she is struck down by its power but is still amazingly calm and quiet, because her husband has made this disease his specialty. He has healed thousands who were similarly afflicted. She isn't troubled in the least because she feels perfectly safe in the hands of one so dear to her – and in whom skill and love are blended in their highest forms. Her faith is reasonable and natural. From every point of view, her husband deserves it from her. This is the kind of faith the happiest of believers exercise toward Christ. There is no physician like Him. No one can save like He can. We love Him, and He loves us. For this reason, we put ourselves into His hands, accept whatever He prescribes, and do whatever He asks. We feel nothing can be out of order while He directs our affairs, because He loves us too much to let us perish (2 Peter 3:9) or suffer a single needless pang.

**Faith is the root of obedience.**

Faith is the root of obedience, which can be clearly seen in the matters of life. When a captain trusts a pilot to steer his vessel into port, he manages the vessel according to the pilot's direction. When a traveler trusts a guide to lead him over a difficult pass, he follows the track his guide points out. When a patient believes in a physician, he carefully follows his prescriptions and directions.

Faith which refuses to obey the commands of the Savior is just a facade and will never save the soul. Jesus gives us directions as to the way of salvation, and if we follow those directions we are saved. Don't forget this. When you trust Jesus, you prove your trust by doing whatever He tells you.

A noteworthy form of faith results from assured knowledge which comes from growth in grace. This is the faith that believes Christ because it knows Him and trusts Him, because it has proved Him to be infallibly faithful. An old Christian woman was in the habit of writing "T&P" in the margin of her Bible whenever she had tried and proved a promise. How easy it is to trust a tried and proven Savior. You may not be able to do this yet, but you will. Everything must have a beginning. In due time, you'll rise to strong faith. This matured faith doesn't ask for signs, but bravely believes.

Look at the faith of the master mariner – I have often marveled at it. He loosens his cable and steams away from the land. For days, weeks, or even months, he never sees sail or shore, and still he goes on day and night without fear, until one morning he finds himself directly opposite the desired haven he'd been steering toward. How does he find his way over the trackless deep? He trusts in his compass, his nautical almanac, his telescope, and the heavenly bodies. Obeying their guidance, without sighting land, he steers so accurately that he doesn't change a point to enter into port. It is a wonderful thing.

Spiritually, it is a blessed thing to totally leave the shores of sight and feeling, and to say good-bye to inward feelings, promising chances, signs, and such things. It is glorious to be far out on the ocean of divine love, believing in God, and steering straight for heaven by the direction of the Word of God. *Blessed are they who did not see, and yet believed* (John 20:29). An abundant entrance will be given to them in the end and a safe voyage on the way. Won't you put your trust in God in Christ Jesus? There I rest with joyous confidence, and I ask you to come with me and believe our Father and our Savior. Come now.

## Chapter 8

# Why Are We Saved by Faith?

W hy is faith the chosen channel of salvation? Without a doubt this is an often-asked question. *For by grace you have been saved through faith* (Ephesians 2:8) is certainly doctrine from Holy Scripture and a decree of God, but why is it? Why is faith selected rather than hope, or love, or patience?

It's fitting for us to be humble in answering such a question, because God's ways aren't always understood, nor are we allowed to presumptuously question them. Humbly we should say that, as far as we can tell, faith has been selected as the channel of grace because faith naturally adapts to being used as the receiver. Think of it this way. If I'm ready to give a poor man a charitable gift, I put it into his hand. Why? Well, it would hardly be fitting to put it into his ear, or to lay it on his foot. The hand is made to receive, and, like the hand of man, faith is created to be a receiver.

Faith that receives Christ is as simple an act as when your child receives an apple from you, because you hold it out and promise to give him the apple if he comes for it. The belief and the receiving relate only to an apple, but they make up precisely the same act as the faith that deals with eternal salvation. What the child's hand is to the apple, your faith is to the perfect salvation of Christ. The child's hand doesn't make the apple, improve the apple, nor deserve the apple. It only receives it.

Faith is chosen by God to be the receiver of salvation, because it doesn't pretend to create salvation nor to help in it. Instead, it's content to humbly receive it. Faith is the tongue that begs pardon, the hand which receives it, and the eye which sees it, but it is not the price which buys it. Faith never makes herself her own plea. Her argument rests on the blood of Christ. She becomes a good servant that brings the riches of the Lord Jesus to the soul, because she acknowledges the source from which she drew them. She admits that grace alone entrusted her with them.

Again, faith is no doubt selected because it gives all the glory to God. It is of faith so it might be by grace, and it is of grace so there might be no boasting, because God can't endure pride. *The haughty He knows from afar* (Psalm 138:6), and He has no wish to come nearer to them. He won't give salvation in a way to suggest or foster pride. Paul says, *Not as a result of works, so that no one may boast* (Ephesians 2:9). Faith excludes all boasting.

The hand which receives charity doesn't say, "I am

to be thanked for accepting the gift." That would be absurd. When the hand lifts bread to the mouth it doesn't say to the body, "Thank me, because I feed you." It is a very simple thing the hand does, but a very necessary thing. It never claims glory for itself for what it does. In the same way, God has selected faith to receive the unspeakable gift of His grace, because it can't take any credit to itself but must adore the gracious God who is the giver of all good. Faith sets the crown on the right head, and therefore the Lord Jesus was to be used to put the crown upon the head of faith, saying, *Your faith has saved you; go in peace* (Luke 7:50).

**Faith saves us because it makes us cling to God and connects us to Him.**

Next, God selects faith as the channel of salvation because it is a sure method which links man with God. When man confides in God, it creates a point that joins the two, and that union guarantees blessing. Faith saves us because it makes us cling to God and connects us to Him. I have often used the following illustration, and I can't think of a better one. It's a story I heard years ago, about a boat that overturned above the falls of Niagara. Two men were being carried down the current, and people on the shore managed to float a rope out to them, which both of the men seized.

One of the men held fast to the rope and was safely drawn to the bank, but the other unwisely let go of the rope when he saw a big log float by. He decided to cling to the log, because it was bigger than the rope and to his thinking the better choice. Sadly, the log with the man on it went right over the falls into the vast abyss, because there was no link – no union – between the log and the shore. The size of the log was of no benefit to the man who grasped it. It needed a connection with the shore to produce safety.

It is the same with the person who trusts in his works, sacraments, ordinances, or anything of that sort. Such a person will not be saved, because there is no connection between him and Christ. But faith, while it might seem like a slender cord, is in the hands of the great God on the shore. Infinite power hauls in the connecting line and pulls the man from destruction. Oh, the blessedness of faith, because it unites us to God.

Faith is also chosen as a conduit of grace because it touches the place where action begins. Even in ordinary things, a certain sort of faith lies at the root of everything. I wonder whether it would be wrong to say we never do anything except through faith of some sort. For instance, if I walk across my study, it is because I believe my legs will carry me. A man eats because he believes in the necessity of food. He goes to work because he believes in the value of money. He accepts a check because he believes the bank will honor it. Columbus discovered America because he believed another continent lay beyond the ocean; and the Pilgrim Fathers colonized it because they believed God would be with them on those rocky shores.

Most great deeds have been born of faith, whether for good or for evil, because faith works wonders through the person in whom it dwells. Faith in its natural form is a persuading force, which enters into all kinds of human actions. Possibly the person who derides faith in God is the person who, in an evil way, has the most faith. In reality, he's fallen into a gullibility which would be ridiculous, if it weren't so disgraceful.

God gives salvation to faith, because by creating faith in us He touches the real mainspring of our emotions and actions. He has, so to speak, taken possession of the battery through which energy is converted and through which He can send the sacred current to every part of our nature. When we believe in Christ and the heart comes into the possession of God, then we are saved from sin and moved toward repentance, holiness, zeal, prayer, and every other gracious thing. It's a consecration from **Love for God is obedience; love for God is holiness.** a common use to a holy use. What oil is to the wheels, what weights are to a clock, what wings are to a bird, what sails are to a ship, that's what faith is to all holy duties and works of the body and mind. Have faith, and all other graces follow and continue to stay on course.

Faith has the power of working through love. It influences the passions toward God, and draws the heart after the best things. He who believes in God will love God without a doubt. Faith is an act of the understanding, but it also proceeds from the heart. *For with the heart a person believes, resulting in righteousness* (Romans 10:10). Therefore God gives salvation to faith because it resides next door to the passions and is closely related to love, and love is the parent and nursemaid of every holy feeling and act. Love for God is obedience; love for God is holiness. To love God and to love man is to be conformed to the image of Christ, and this is salvation.

Similarly, faith creates peace and joy. The one who has faith rests in Christ and is tranquil. They are glad and joyous, which is training for heaven. God gives all heavenly gifts to faith for this reason among others – that faith works in us the life and spirit which are to be eternally displayed in heaven above. Faith furnishes us with armor for this life (Ephesians 6:10-18), and teaches us about the life to come. It enables believers to live and to die without fear, and it prepares us for action and for suffering. The Lord also selects it as a most convenient medium for conveying grace to us and thereby positioning us for glory.

Faith certainly does for us what nothing else can do. It gives us joy and peace and causes us to stop striving and to enter into rest (Psalm 46:10). Why do people attempt to gain salvation by other means? An old preacher says, "A silly servant who is told to open a door, sets his shoulder to it and pushes with all his might. But the door doesn't budge. He can't enter, even when he uses all his strength. Another comes along with a key, easily unlocks the door, and enters right in. Those who hope to be saved by works are pushing at heaven's gate without result. Faith is the key which opens the gate instantly."

Won't you use that key? The Lord commands you to believe in His dear Son, and in doing so, you will live. Isn't this the promise of the gospel? *He who has believed and has been baptized shall be saved* (Mark 16:16). How can you object to a way of salvation which entrusts itself to the mercy and wisdom of our gracious God?

# Chapter 9

# Alas! I Can Do Nothing Good!

After the anxious heart has accepted the doctrine of atonement and learned the great truth that salvation is by faith in the Lord Jesus, it is often deeply troubled with a sense of inability to do what is good. Many groan that they can do nothing good. They aren't making an excuse, but are expressing a daily burden. They wholeheartedly would do good, if they could, but each one can honestly say, *the willing is present in me, but the doing of the good is not* (Romans 7:18).

This feeling seems to make the gospel null and void, because what's the use of food to a hungry man if he can't get at it? What benefit is the river of the water of life if one can't drink? This brings to mind the story of the doctor and the poor woman's child. The wise practitioner told the mother that her little one would soon get better under proper treatment, but it was absolutely necessary for her boy to regularly drink the best wine and spend some time at one of the German spas. Remember, this was said to a widow who could hardly get bread to eat. In the same way, it sometimes seems to the troubled heart that the simple gospel of "believe and live" isn't so simple after all, because it asks the poor sinner to do what he cannot do. To the truly spiritually awakened but half-instructed believer, there appears to be a missing link. For them, they can see the salvation of Jesus in the distance, but how is it to be reached? The soul is without strength, and doesn't know what to do. It lies within sight of the city of refuge and can't enter its gate.

Is this lack of strength provided for in the plan of salvation? It is. The work of the Lord is perfect. It begins where we are, and asks nothing of us in order to reach its completion. When the good Samaritan saw the traveler lying wounded and half-dead, he didn't tell him to get up and come to him, and mount the donkey and ride off to the inn. No, *came upon him* (Luke 10:33), ministered to him, lifted him onto the beast, and carried him to the inn. That's how the Lord Jesus deals with us in our low and wretched condition.

We have seen that God justifies – that He justifies the ungodly – and that He justifies them through faith in the precious blood of Jesus. Now we must look at the condition these ungodly people are in when Jesus works out their salvation. Many people who are spiritually awakened aren't troubled about only their sin but also about their moral weakness. They have no strength to escape from the deep mud into which they have fallen, or even the strength to keep out of it later. They not only grieve over what they have done, but also over what they can't do. They feel powerless, helpless, and spiritually lifeless.

It may sound odd to say that they feel dead, and yet on some level it is true, because in their own eyes they are incapable of all good. They feel they can't travel the road to heaven, because their bones are broken. None of the men of strength have found their hands (Psalm 76:5); in fact, they are without **Our helplessness is extreme.** strength. However, we don't need to look to our own strength, because we can happily see the mention of God's love to us written in His Word. *For while we were still helpless, at the right time Christ died for the ungodly* (Romans 5:6).

In this verse, we see conscious helplessness relieved – relieved by the Lord's intervention. Our helplessness is extreme. It isn't written, "When we were comparatively weak Christ died for us," or, "When we had only a little strength," but rather the description is absolute and unrestricted: *While we were still helpless.* We had no strength whatsoever which could help in our salvation. Our Lord's words were emphatically true. *Apart from Me you can do nothing* (John 15:5). I can go further and remind you of the great love with which the Lord loved us, *even when we were dead in our transgressions* (Ephesians 2:5). To be dead is even more than being without strength.

The one thing that the poor sinner lacking strength has to fix his mind on and firmly remember as his one ground of hope, is the divine assurance that He *at the right time died for the ungodly.* Believe this and all hopelessness will disappear. As in the story of the fabled Midas who turned everything into gold by his touch, so it is with true faith – it turns everything it touches into good. Our needs and weaknesses become blessings when faith deals with them.

Let's consider specific forms of this lack of strength. To begin with, one person will say, "I don't seem to have the strength to collect my thoughts and keep them fixed on those serious topics which concern my salvation. Even a short prayer is almost too much for me. Perhaps this is partly due to natural weakness, partly because I've harmed myself through over-indulgence, and partly because I worry myself with worldly cares to the point that I'm not capable of the important thoughts necessary before a soul can be saved."

This happens to be a very common form of sinful weakness as many others experience this same lack of strength. They can't keep their minds focused on uninterrupted sequential thinking to save their lives. Many poor men and women are illiterate and uneducated, and they find deep thought to be hard work. Others are so light and trifling by nature that they can't follow a long process of argument and reasoning any more than they can fly. They can never comprehend a profound mystery even if they spend their whole life in the effort.

The fact is, you don't need to despair because continuous thought isn't what's necessary for salvation, but rather a simple reliance upon Jesus. Hold on to this one fact: *At the right time Christ died for the ungodly.* This truth will not require any deep research or profound reasoning or convincing argument from you. Just stand on this truth. Fix your mind on it and rest there.

Let this one great, kind, and glorious fact lie in your spirit until it perfumes all your thoughts and makes you rejoice even though you are without strength. See the Lord Jesus as your strength and your song, for He has become your salvation. According to the Scriptures, it is a revealed fact that *at the right time Christ died for the ungodly* when they were still without strength. You may have heard these words hundreds of times, and yet you've never perceived their meaning. There's an uplifting aroma about them, isn't there? Jesus didn't die for our righteousness but died for our sins. He didn't come to save us because we were worth saving, but because we were utterly worthless, ruined, and undone. He didn't come to earth because of anything we've done to merit His love, but solely for reasons which He fetched from the depths of His own divine love (Romans 5:8). In His time He died for those whom He describes, not as godly, but as ungodly.

**See the Lord Jesus as your strength and your song.**

Even if your mind is limited in its understanding, it can grasp this truth. Hold on to it, for it is able to cheer the heaviest heart. Let this verse lie under your tongue like a sweet morsel, until it dissolves into your heart and flavors all your thoughts. Then it won't matter much even if our thoughts are as scattered as autumn leaves. People who have never been brilliant in science, or have displayed little originality in their thinking, have been fully able to accept the doctrine of the cross and have been saved. Why shouldn't you?

I've heard another man say, "My lack of strength lies mainly in the fact that I can't repent sufficiently!" People's ideas of what repentance is are often curious. Many imagine many tears should be shed, many groans heaved, and much despair endured. Where does this unreasonable notion come from? Unbelief and despair are sins. Therefore, I don't see how they can be fundamental elements of acceptable repentance. Still, many regard them as necessary parts of the true Christian experience, but this is greatly inaccurate.

However, I know what they mean, because in the days of my spiritual darkness I felt the same way. I wanted to repent, but I thought I couldn't do it. And yet even while I was thinking this, I was actually repenting. Odd as it may sound, I felt that I couldn't feel. I used to get into a corner and weep because I couldn't weep. And I fell into bitter grief because I didn't sorrow enough for sin. What a jumble it all is when, in our unbelieving state, we begin to judge our own condition. It is like a blind man looking at his own eyes. My heart was melted within me for fear, because I thought my heart was as hard as an unyielding stone. My heart was broken to think it wouldn't break. Now I can see that I was exhibiting the very thing I thought I didn't possess, but then I didn't know where I was spiritually.

Oh, how I wish I could help others into the light I now enjoy. It would make me so happy to say anything which might shorten the time of their confusion – if I could say a few simple words and pray *the Helper, the Holy Spirit* (John 14:26) would apply them to the heart. Remember that the person who truly repents is never satisfied with his own repentance. We can't repent perfectly any more than we can live perfectly. No matter how pure our tears are, there will always be some dirt in them, because we always have something to be repented of even in our greatest sorrow or deepest contrition for sin.

But listen! To repent is to change your mind about sin and Christ, and all the countless things about God. Sorrow is implied in repentance, but the main point is the turning of the heart from sin to Christ. If this turning happens, you have the substance of true repentance, even if no outcry and no despair ever casts a shadow upon your mind. If you can't repent like you should, if you firmly believe

> **Sorrow is implied in repentance, but the main point is the turning of the heart from sin to Christ.**

that *at the right time Christ died for the ungodly*, it will really help you to do so. Meditate on this again and again. How can you continue to be hard-hearted when you know that out of supreme love Christ *died for the ungodly*? Let me persuade you to reason within yourself like this: As ungodly as I am, even though my heart of steel won't yield, since He *died for the ungodly*, He still died for people like me. Help me to believe this and feel the power of it upon my flinty heart.

Blot out every other reflection from your soul, and sit down with the Lord and meditate deeply on this one stunning display of unmerited, unexpected, unparalleled love: Christ died for the ungodly. Read over the account of the Lord's death carefully in the four Gospels. If anything can melt your stubborn heart, it will be the sufferings of Jesus and the fact that He suffered all this for His enemies.

> *O Jesus, sweet the tears I shed,*
> *While at Thy cross I kneel,*
> *Gaze on Thy wounded, fainting head,*
> *And all Thy sorrows feel.*
>
> *My heart dissolves to see Thee bleed,*
> *This heart so hard before;*
> *I hear Thee for the guilty plead,*
> *And grief o'erflows the more.*
>
> *'Twas for the sinful Thou didst die,*
> *And I a sinner stand;*
> *What love speaks from Thy dying eye,*
> *And from each pierced hand!*
> – Ray Palmer

If you understand the full meaning of the divine sacrifice of Jesus, you must repent of ever being opposed to One so full of love. It is written, *they will look on Me whom they have pierced; and they will mourn for Him, as one mourns for an only son, and they will weep bitterly over Him like the bitter weeping over a firstborn* (Zechariah 12:10). Repentance won't make you see Christ, but seeing Christ will give you repentance. You can't make a Christ out of your repentance, but you must look for repentance which brings you to Christ. As the Holy Spirit turns us to Christ, He turns us from sin. Look away from the effect to the cause, from your own repenting to the Lord Jesus who is exalted on high to give repentance.

I heard another say, "I am tormented with horrible thoughts. Wherever I go, blasphemies sneak up on me. Frequently at my work, a dreadful suggestion forces its way into my thoughts, and even in the night, I'm startled from my sleep by whispers of the Evil One. I can't get away from this horrible temptation."

I can relate to such torment, because I've been hunted by this wolf. A man might as well hope to fight a swarm of flies with a sword as to master his own thoughts when they are attacked by the Devil. A poor tempted soul assailed by satanic suggestions is like a traveler I read about whose head, ears, and whole body were attacked by a swarm of angry bees. He couldn't keep them off or escape from them. They stung him everywhere and threatened to be the death of him. It's no wonder you feel you don't have the strength to stop these hideous and abominable thoughts which Satan pours into your soul. But again I remind you of the Scripture before us – *For while we were still helpless, at the right time Christ died for the ungodly.* Jesus knew where we were and where we would be. He saw we couldn't overcome the prince of the power of the air. He knew we would be greatly worried by him; but even then, when He saw us in that condition, Christ *died for the ungodly.*

Cast the anchor of your faith on this. The Devil himself can't tell you that you're not ungodly, so believe that Jesus died for you just the way you are. Remember the way Martin Luther cut the Devil's head off with his own sword:

"Oh," said the Devil to Martin Luther, "you are a sinner."

"Yes," Luther answered. "Christ died to save sinners."

In this way, he slashed him with his own sword. Hide yourself in this knowledge – this refuge – and stay there. *At the right time Christ died for the ungodly.* If you stand in that truth, the blasphemous thoughts you don't have the strength to drive away will go away by themselves, because Satan will see that he is accomplishing nothing by plaguing you with them. If you hate these thoughts, they are not yours but are injected into your thinking by the Devil. In that case, he is responsible and not you. If you strive against them, they are no more yours than the cursing and lies of rioters in the street. The Devil means to drive you to despair by such thoughts or to at least keep you from trusting Jesus.

> Cast yourself on Him, thoughts and all, and see if He isn't mighty enough to save.

The poor diseased woman couldn't come to Jesus because of the press of the crowd (Mark 5:24-29), and you're in much the same situation as the rush and throng of these dreadful thoughts press in on you. Still, she put forth her finger and touched the fringe of the Lord's garment, and she was healed. Do the same. Jesus died for those who are guilty of *all manner of sin and blasphemy.* Based on this truth, I'm sure He won't refuse those who are unwillingly the captives of evil thoughts. Cast yourself on Him, thoughts and all, and see if He isn't mighty enough to save. He can quiet those horrible whisperings of the Devil, or He can enable you to see them in their true light so they no longer worry you. In His own way, He can and will save you and after a time give you perfect peace. Only trust Him for this and everything else.

That form of inability which lies in a supposed lack of power to believe is sadly perplexing because we aren't strangers to the cry:

> *Oh, that I could believe,*
> *Then all would easy be;*
> *I would, but cannot; Lord, relieve,*
> *My help must come from thee.*

Many remain in the dark spiritually for years because they say they have no power, but in actuality what they need to do is give up all their own power and rest in the power of another – the Lord Jesus.

It is a very curious thing, this whole matter of believing, because people don't get much help by *trying* to believe. Believing doesn't come by trying. If a person made a statement about something that happened today, I wouldn't tell him that I would try to believe him. If I believed in the truthfulness of the man who told me about the incident he saw, I would instantly accept what he said. If I didn't think him to be a true man, I would not believe him, but there would be no trying in the matter. Now, when God declares that there is salvation in Christ Jesus, I must either believe Him at once, or make Him a liar. Surely you won't hesitate as to which is the right path in this case. The witness of God must be true, and we are bound to believe in Jesus when we hear this truth.

Perhaps you've been trying too hard to believe. Don't aim at having great faith, but be satisfied with having a faith you can hold in your hand with this one truth: *For while we were still helpless, at the right time Christ died for the ungodly.* He laid down His life for us while we as yet didn't believe in Him, nor were we able to believe in Him. He died for us, not as believers but as sinners. He came to make sinners into believers and saints, but when He died for us He could see we were utterly without strength.

If you hold to the truth that Christ died for the ungodly and believe it, your faith will save you and you can go in peace. If you trust your soul to Jesus, who died for the ungodly, even though you can't believe all things, or move mountains, or do any other miraculous works, you are still saved. It isn't great faith but true faith that saves, and the salvation lies not in the faith, but in the Christ in whom faith trusts. Faith like a grain of mustard seed will bring salvation (Matthew 17:20). It isn't the measure of faith but the sincerity of faith which is to be considered. A person can surely believe what he knows to be true, and as you know Jesus to be true, you, my friend, can believe in Him.

The cross which is the object of faith is also, by the power of the Holy Spirit, the cause of it. Sit down and watch the dying Savior until faith springs up spontaneously in your heart. No place creates confidence like Calvary. The air of that sacred hill brings health to trembling faith. Many who look to the cross have said:

*While I view Thee,*
*    wounded, grieving,*
*Breathless, on the cursed tree,*
*    [Gladly] I'd feel my heart believing*
*Thou didst suffer thus for me.*

Another person says, "Sadly, my lack of strength rests in the fact that I can't quit my sin, and I know I can't go to heaven and carry my sin with me."

I'm glad you know that, because it is true. You must be divorced from your sin, or you can't be married to Christ. While on the playing field on a Sabbath, a question flashed into the mind of the young John Bunyan: "Will you hold on to your sins and go to hell, or will you quit your sins and go to heaven?" This question

> You must be divorced from your sin, or you can't be married to Christ.

brought him to a dead standstill. It's a question we all have to answer, because we can't go on in sin and go to heaven. You must quit sin or quit hope. What's your reply? "Yes, I'm willing enough, *for the willing is present in me, but the doing of the good is not* (Romans 7:18). Sin masters me, and I have no strength." Even if you have no strength, remember that this verse is still true, for *while we were still helpless, at the right time Christ died for the ungodly.* Can you still believe this even when other things seem to contradict it? The real question is, will you believe it?

God has said it, and it's a fact. Therefore, hold on to this truth and don't let go, because your only hope lies in God's truth. Believe this – trust Jesus, and you will soon find the power to slay your sin; but apart from Him, the armed strongman (the Devil) will hold you as his bond slave forever.

Personally, I could never have overcome my sinfulness on my own. I tried and failed. My evil propensities were too many until, through the belief that Christ died for me, I cast my guilty soul on Him. When I did that, I received a conquering truth by which I overcame my sinful self. The doctrine of the cross can be used to slay sin in the same way the old warriors used their huge two-handed swords and mowed down their enemies with every stroke. There's nothing like faith in Jesus, for it overcomes all evil. If Christ died for me, ungodly as I am, without strength just like I am, then I can't live in sin any longer but must arouse myself to love and serve Him who has redeemed me (Galatians 3:13-14). I can't flirt with the evil which slew my best friend, Jesus. I must be holy for His sake, because how can I live in sin when He has died to save me from it?

See what a marvelous help this offers those who are without strength – to know and believe that *at the right time Christ died for the ungodly* ones like you. Have you accepted this knowledge yet?

It is difficult for our darkened, prejudiced, and unbelieving minds to see the heart of the gospel (Ephesians 4:18). At times, while I've been preaching, I've thought that I laid down the gospel so clearly that it couldn't be more plain. Yet I have sensed that even intelligent hearers have failed to understand what was meant by *Turn to Me and be saved* (Isaiah 45:22). Converts usually say that they didn't know the gospel till such and such a day, and yet they'd heard it for years. The gospel is unknown, not from lack of explanation but from absence of personal revelation. The Holy Spirit is ready to give this revelation to those who ask Him, and when it is given, the sum total of the truth is revealed within these words: Christ died for the ungodly.

Another common regret I hear is, "My weakness is that once I'm impressed by the Word on Sunday, I don't seem to keep hold to that viewpoint. Throughout the week, I meet with an evil companion and my good feelings disappear. My co-workers don't believe in anything and say such terrible things that I don't know how to answer them. So I find myself knocked off my feet."

I understand adapting to new situations like this very well, and I tremble for people like this. At the same time, if such a person is really sincere, his weakness can be met by divine grace. The Holy Spirit can cast out the evil spirit of the fear of man and make the coward brave. You must not remain in this vacillating state, because it won't do you any good to have such little regard for yourself. Stand up straight and take a good look at yourself. Were you meant to be like a toad under a harrow, afraid for your life whether you move or stand still? Aren't you capable of independent opinion or action?

**The Holy Spirit can cast out the evil spirit of the fear of man and make the coward brave.**

I would do many things to please my friends, but to go to hell to please them is more than I would offer or volunteer. While it might keep us on good terms with our fellow man, it's not worth it to lose the friendship of

JESUS CAME TO SAVE SINNERS

God. A man who struggles with this may say, "I know that, but still, even though I know it, I can't find the courage. I can't stand firm." Well, again I'd offer the same verse. *For while we were still helpless, at the right time Christ died for the ungodly.* If Peter were here, he would say, "The Lord Jesus died for me even when I was such a poor weak creature that the maid who kept the fire drove me to lie and to swear that I didn't know the Lord" (Mark 14:66-72).

Yes, Jesus died for those who forsook Him and fled. Firmly take hold of this truth – that Christ died for the ungodly while they were still without strength. This is your way out of your cowardice. Get it driven into your soul, "Christ died for me," and you'll soon be ready to die for Him. Believe it. He suffered in your place and offered full, true, and satisfactory payment for you (1 Corinthians 6:20). If you believe this fact, you will be forced to feel that you can't be ashamed of Him who died for you.

Full conviction that this is true will embolden you with dauntless courage. Look at the believers in the early days of Christianity, when this great thought of Christ's exceeding love was vibrant and fresh in the church. People weren't only ready to die, but they also grew determined to suffer and even presented themselves by hundreds at the judgment seats of the rulers, confessing the Christ. I don't say that they were wise to court a cruel death; but it proves my point, that a sense of the love of Jesus lifts the mind above all fear of what man can do to us. Why shouldn't it produce the same effect in you? I pray that it might now inspire you with a brave resolve to show yourself on the Lord's side and to be His follower to the end.

May the Holy Spirit help us to come by faith in the Lord Jesus, and in this way, it will be well.

# Chapter 10

# The Increase of Faith

How can we obtain increased faith? This is a sincere question for many people, including the apostles (Luke 17:5). People want to believe but can't. You can find a great deal of nonsense on this subject, so let's be strictly practical in our dealing with it. Common sense is needed in religion as much as anywhere else, so let's start with the question, "What am I to do in order to believe?"

One who was asked the best way to do a certain simple act replied that the best way to do it was to do it at once. We waste time in discussing methods when the action is simple. The shortest way to believe is to believe. If the Holy Spirit has made you open, you will believe as soon as truth is set before you. You will believe it because it is true. The gospel command is clear. *Believe in the Lord Jesus, and you will be saved* (Acts 16:31). It is pointless to avoid this with questions and quibbles because the order is plain. So let it be obeyed.

If you have difficulty, be still and take it before God in prayer (Psalm 46:10). Tell the great Father exactly what puzzles you and beg Him by His Holy Spirit to solve the question. If I can't believe a statement in a book, I'm happy to contact the author and ask what he means by it. If he is a sincere man, his explanation will satisfy me.

How much more will the divine explanation of the hard points of Scripture satisfy the heart of the true seeker? The Lord is willing to make Himself known. Go to Him and see if it isn't so. Retreat immediately to your prayer closet, and cry, "O Holy Spirit, lead me into the truth. What I don't know, You teach me."

**If you have difficulty, be still and take it before God in prayer.**

Additionally, if faith seems difficult, it's possible that God the Holy Spirit will enable you to believe if you frequently and earnestly hear what you are commanded to believe. We believe many things because we have heard them so often. Don't you find that the case in everyday life? If you hear something fifty times a day, don't you eventually come to believe it?

Some people have come to believe very implausible statements in this way. Therefore, I don't wonder that the good Spirit often blesses this method of frequent hearing of the truth and uses it to work faith concerning what is to be believed. It is written, *faith comes from hearing* (Romans 10:17); therefore, hear often. If I sincerely and attentively hear the gospel, one of these days I will find myself believing that which I hear, through the blessed operation of the Spirit of God upon my mind. Only be sure that you hear the gospel, and don't distract your mind with either hearing or reading things designed to make you stagger or stumble.

Next, I also recommend you consider the testimony of others. The Samaritans believed because of what the woman at the well told them concerning Jesus. Many of our beliefs arise out of the testimony of others. I believe the country of Japan exists even though I have never seen it. I believe because others have been there. I believe I will die, even though I've never died, because a great many people I once knew have done so. Therefore, I have a conviction that I will die too. The testimony of many convinces me of that fact.

In the same way, listen to those who tell you how they were saved, how they were pardoned, how their character changed. If you look into the matter, you'll find somebody just like you has been saved. If you've lived as a thief, you'll find a thief who rejoiced to wash away his sin in the fountain of Christ's blood. If you've lived an immoral life, you'll find that men and women who have fallen in that way are now cleansed and changed. If you are in depression, just inquire a little among God's people and you'll discover believers who have struggled with depression in the same way at times, and they will be pleased to tell you how the Lord delivered them. As you listen to one account after another of those who have tried the Word of God and proved it, the divine Spirit will lead you to believe.

Did you heard about the African who was told by the missionary that water sometimes becomes so hard that a man can walk on it? The African declared that he believed a great many things the missionary told him, but he would never believe that. When he came to England, it came to pass that one frosty day he saw the river frozen, but he wouldn't venture onto it. He knew it was a deep river and felt certain he would drown if he dared risk it. He couldn't be coaxed to walk out onto the frozen water until his friend and many others stepped out onto the frozen surface. Seeing others safely venture onto the ice, he was persuaded and trusted he could do the same. So, as you see others believe in the Lamb of God and detect their joy and peace, you'll be gently led to believe. The experience of others is one of God's ways of helping us to faith. You either have to believe in Jesus and receive life or remain spiritually dead in your sin. There's no hope for you but in Him.

**You either have to believe in Jesus and receive life or remain spiritually dead in your sin.**

Here's an even better idea: take note of the authority by which you are commanded to believe and it will significantly help you to faith. The authority isn't mine, or you might as well reject it. But you are commanded to believe on the authority of God Himself. He tells you to believe in Jesus Christ (Acts 16:31), and you must not refuse to obey your Maker.

The foreman of a certain business had often heard the gospel but was troubled with the fear that he might not truly know Christ. One day he received a note from his good boss which said, "Come to my house immediately after work." The foreman appeared at his boss's door and the boss came out and said somewhat roughly, "What do you want, John, troubling me at this time? Work is done; what right have you to come here?"

"Sir," he said, "I received a card from you saying I was to come here after work."

"Do you mean to say that just because you received a card from me you have the right to come to my house and call on me after business hours?"

"I don't understand what you mean," replied the foreman. "It seems to me that, since you sent for me, I had a right to come."

"Come in, John," said his boss. "I have another message I want to read to you." The two of them stepped inside and he sat down and read these words from the Bible: *Come to Me, all who are weary and heavy-laden, and I will give you rest* (Matthew 11:28). His boss looked at him and said, "Do you think after such a message from Christ that you can be wrong in coming to Him?" The poor foreman saw it instantly and believed in the Lord Jesus for eternal life, because he finally understood that he had good reason and authority for believing. And so do you. You have good authority for coming to Christ, because the Lord himself tells you to trust Him.

If that doesn't produce faith in you, think over what it is that you must believe – that the Lord Jesus Christ suffered in the place of sinners and is able to save all who trust Him. This is the most blessed fact people have ever been told to believe. It's the most agreeable, the most comforting, the most divine truth ever set before mortal minds. I advise you to think about it much and to search out the grace and love it contains.

Study the four Gospels, study Paul's epistles, and see if the message isn't such a credible one that you are forced to believe it.

If that doesn't do it for you, then think about the person of Jesus Christ. Think about who He is, what He did, where He is, and what He is. How can you doubt Him? It is heartless to distrust the ever-truthful Jesus. He's done nothing to deserve distrust. On the contrary, it should be easy for us to rely on Him. Why crucify Him all over again by unbelief? Isn't this like crowning Him with thorns and spitting on Him again? Why isn't He to be trusted? The soldiers made Him a martyr, but you, by your unbelief, make Him a liar; this is far worse. Don't ask, "How can I believe?" Instead ask, "How can I disbelieve?"

> Don't ask, "How can I believe?" Instead ask, "How can I disbelieve?"

If none of these things brings you to the truth, then something is totally wrong. My last word of advice is to submit yourself to God. You are a rebel, a proud rebel, and that is why you don't believe your God. Prejudice or pride is at the bottom of your unbelief. May the Spirit of God take away your opposition toward Him and make you surrender to Him. Give up your rebellion, throw down your defenses, yield your will, and surrender to your King. When a soul throws up its hands in hopelessness and cries, "Lord, I surrender," before long, faith becomes easy.

The reason you can't believe is because you still have a quarrel with God and a determination to have your own will and own way. Christ said, *How can you believe, when you receive glory from one another?* (John 5:44). A proud self creates unbelief. Submit – yield to your God and you will agreeably believe in your Savior. I pray that the Holy Spirit will now work secretly but effectually within you, and at this very moment bring you to believe in the Lord Jesus. Amen.

# Chapter 11

# Regeneration and the Holy Spirit

*Unless one is born again he cannot see the kingdom of God* (John 3:3). This word of our Lord Jesus seems like a flame blocking the way of many, like the drawn sword of the cherub at the gate of paradise (Genesis 3:24). Such people have despaired, because this change is beyond anything they can do in their own effort. The new birth is from above and therefore not in man's power. Now, it's the furthest thing from my mind to deny or to ever conceal a truth in order to create a false sense of comfort. I freely admit the new birth is supernatural, and that it can't be worked out by the sinner's own efforts. If I were wicked enough to try to cheer you by persuading you to reject or forget what is unquestionably true, such help would be flawed.

But isn't it remarkable that the very chapter in

which our Lord makes this sweeping declaration also contains the most explicit statement as to salvation by faith? Read the third chapter of John's gospel and don't just dwell on its earlier sentences. It is true that the third verse says, *Jesus answered and said to him, Truly, truly, I say to you, unless one is born again he cannot see the kingdom of God.* But then, the fourteenth and fifteenth verses go on to say, *As Moses lifted up the serpent in the wilderness, even so must the Son of Man be lifted up; so that whoever believes will in Him have eternal life.* Then verse 18 repeats the same doctrine in the broadest terms:

> *He who believes in Him is not judged;*
> *he who does not believe has been judged*
> *already, because he has not believed in the*
> *name of the only begotten Son of God.*

It is clear that these two statements must agree, since they came from the same lips, and are recorded in the same inspired chapter. Why would we create a difficulty where none exists? If one statement assures us of the necessity of salvation as something only God can give, and if another assures us that the Lord will save us upon our believing in Jesus, then we can safely conclude that the Lord will give to those who believe all that is declared to be essential to salvation. In fact, the Lord produces the new birth in all who believe in Jesus, and their believing is the surest evidence that they are born again.

We trust in Jesus because we can't do it ourselves. If it was in our own power, what need would we have to look to Him? It is our part to believe, and it's the Lord's part to create us anew. He will not believe for us, and we aren't to do the regenerating work for Him. It is enough for us to obey the gracious command, and it's for the Lord to work the new birth in us (Philippians 2:13). He who would go so far as to die on the cross for us can and will give us all things we need for our eternal security.

A saving change of heart is the work of the Holy Spirit (Titus 3:5), so don't venture to question or forget it. The work of the Holy Spirit is secret and mysterious and can only be perceived by its results. Mysteries about our natural birth could be a secular curiosity to pry into, and that's even more the case with the sacred workings of the Spirit of God. *The wind blows where it wishes and you hear the sound of it, but do not know where it comes from and where it is going; so is everyone who is born of the Spirit* (John 3:8). However, this much we do know: the mysterious work of the Holy Spirit can't be a reason for refusing to believe in Jesus to whom that same Spirit bears witness.

> A saving change of heart is the work of the Holy Spirit.

For example, if a person was asked to sow seed in a field and he didn't do it, he couldn't excuse his neglect by saying, "It would be useless to sow unless God caused the seed to grow." In other words, he wouldn't be justified in ignoring the plowing because the secret energy of God alone can create a harvest.

No one is hindered in the ordinary activities of life. Scripture says that unless the Lord builds the house, they labor in vain that build it, but notice that they do labor (Psalm 127:1). Those who believe in Jesus will find that the Holy Spirit never refuses to work in them. In fact, his believing is the proof that the Spirit is already at work in his heart.

God works in providence – preparing for the future, but because He does so doesn't mean people should sit still and do nothing. Without God's divine power giving them life and strength, they couldn't move, and yet they go on their way without considering the power being granted by Him from day to day – Him in whose hand their breath and all their ways are held. It is the same in grace. We repent and believe, but if the Lord didn't enable us, we could do neither. We forsake sin and trust in Jesus, and then we recognize that *it is God who is at work in you, both to will and to work for His good pleasure* (Philippians 2:13). It is pointless to pretend there is any real difficulty in the matter.

> Scripture says that unless the Lord builds the house, they labor in vain that build it, but notice that they do labor.

Some truths which are hard to explain in words are simple enough in actual experience. No discrepancy exists between the truth that the sinner believes and that his faith functions within him by the Holy Spirit. Only foolishness can lead people to confuse themselves about simple matters while their souls are in danger. No one would refuse to enter a lifeboat because he didn't understand the specific weight of bodies. Nor would a starving man refuse to eat until he understood the whole process of nutrition.

If you won't believe until you can understand all

the mysteries of faith, you will never be saved. And if you allow self-invented difficulties to keep you from accepting forgiveness through your Lord and Savior, you will die condemned, which will be totally deserved. Don't commit spiritual suicide through a passion for discussing abstract subtleties.

Chapter 12

# I Know My Redeemer Lives

I have continually spoken to you concerning Christ crucified, who is the great hope of the guilty, but it is wise to remember that our Lord has risen from the dead and lives eternally. You aren't asked to trust in a dead Jesus, but in One who, though He died for our sins, has risen again for our justification. You can go to Jesus as to a living and present friend. He isn't just a memory, but a person continually present who will hear your prayers and answer them. He lives intentionally to carry on the work for which He once laid down His life. He is interceding for sinners at the right hand of the Father, and, for this reason, He is able to save those who come to God by Him. Come and experience this living Savior, if you have never done so before.

This living Jesus is also raised to renowned glory and power. He doesn't mourn or suffer like a humble man before his foes, or work as the carpenter's son.

Instead, He is exalted *far above all rule and authority and power and dominion, and every name that is named* (Ephesians 1:21). The Father has given Him all power in heaven and on earth, and He exercises this important attribute in carrying out His work of grace. Hear what Peter and the other apostles testified concerning Him before the high priest and the council:

> *The God of our fathers raised up Jesus,*
> *whom you had put to death by hanging*
> *Him on a cross. He is the one whom God*
> *exalted to His right hand as a Prince and*
> *a Savior, to grant repentance to Israel, and*
> *forgiveness of sins.* (Acts 5:30-31)

The glory which surrounds the ascended Lord should breathe hope into every believer's heart. Jesus is no average person – He is a Savior and a great one. He is the crowned and enthroned Redeemer of men. The sovereign right over life and death is vested in Him. The Father has made Him Mediator to all people under the mediatorial government of the Son, so that He can make alive whom He will. He *opens and no one will shut, and who shuts and no one opens* (Revelation 3:7). The soul which is bound by the cords of sin and condemnation can be loosened by His Word in a moment. He stretches out the power of the truth and whosoever touches it lives. It's good for us that just like sin lives, the flesh lives, and the Devil lives – so Jesus lives. It's also good that whatever power these can have to ruin us, Jesus has still greater power to save us.

All His exaltation and ability are on our account.

He is exalted "to be" and "to give." He is exalted to be a Prince and Savior so He can give all that is needed to accomplish the salvation of all who come under His rule. Jesus holds nothing back – there's nothing He won't use for a sinner's salvation and nothing He won't use to display His overflowing grace. He links His position as Prince with His Saviorship as if He couldn't have the one without the other. He establishes His exaltation, which is designed to bring blessings to people, as if it were the flower and crown of His glory. Could anything be more calculated to raise the hopes of seeking sinners who are looking toward Christ?

Jesus endured great humiliation. Due to this, there was room for Him to be exalted. By that humiliation, He accomplished and endured all the Father's will and was rewarded by being raised to glory. He uses that exaltation on behalf of His people. Raise your eyes to these hills of glory, from whence your help must come (Psalm 121:1). Contemplate the high glories of the Prince and Savior. Isn't it most promising for people that a Man is now on the throne of the universe? Isn't it glorious that the Lord of all is the Savior of sinners? We have a friend in the court of God, a friend on the throne. He will use all His influence for those who entrust their concerns to His hands. One of our poets, Isaac Watts, sings it well in the hymn "He Ever Lives to Intercede Before His Father's Face":

> We have a friend in the court of God, a friend on the throne.

*He ever lives to intercede*
*    Before His Father's face:*
*Give Him, my soul,*
*    Thy cause to plead,*
*No doubt the Father's grace.*

Friend, commit your cause and your case to those once-pierced hands, which are now glorified with the signet rings of royal power and honor. No case ever failed which was left with this great advocate.

## Chapter 13

# Repentance Must Go with Forgiveness

It is clear from the verses we've already looked at that repentance is bound up with the forgiveness of sins. In Acts 5:31 we read that Jesus is *exalted . . . as a Prince and a Savior, to grant repentance to Israel, and forgiveness of sins*. These two blessings come from that sacred hand once nailed to the cross but now raised to glory. Repentance and forgiveness are riveted together by the eternal purpose of God. *What shall we say then? Are we to continue in sin so that grace may increase? May it never be! How shall we who died to sin still live in it?* (Romans 6:1-2).

Repentance must go with forgiveness. If you just think about this a little, you'll see it is so. Pardon of sin can't be given to an unrepentant sinner. This would settle him in his evil ways and teach him to think nothing of evil. If the Lord were to say, "You love sin and live in it, and you are going on from bad to worse, but, all the same, I forgive you," this would proclaim a horrible license for wickedness. The foundations of social order would be eliminated and moral disorder would follow. I can't begin to tell you what innumerable mischiefs would certainly occur if repentance could be separated from forgiveness and could pass by the sin while the sinner remained as fond of it as ever.

As you would expect, if we believe in the holiness of God but continue in our sin and won't repent of it, we can't be forgiven but must reap the consequence of our obstinacy. According to the infinite goodness of God, we are promised that if we forsake our sins and confess them and by faith accept the grace provided in Christ Jesus, God is faithful and just to forgive us our sins, and to cleanse us from all unrighteousness (1 John 1:9). But, so long as God lives, there can be no promise of mercy to those who continue in their evil ways and refuse to acknowledge their wrongdoing. Surely, no rebel can expect the king to pardon his treason while he remains in open revolt. No one can be so foolish as to imagine that the judge of all the earth will put away our sins if we refuse to put them away ourselves.

This is how it must be for the fullness of divine mercy. Mercy which forgives the sin and still lets the sinner live in it would be limited and superficial. It would be perverted mercy and unsatisfactory. Which do you think is the greater benefit, cleansing from the guilt of sin or deliverance from the power of sin? I won't attempt to weigh two such surpassing mercies in the scales. Neither of them could come to us apart from the precious blood of Jesus. But, if a comparison has to be drawn, it seems to me that being delivered from the dominion of sin, to be made holy, to be made like God, must be considered the greater of the two. To be forgiven is a favor beyond measure.

We make this one of the first notes of our psalm of praise: *Who pardons all your iniquities* (Psalm 103:3). But if we could be forgiven and then permitted to love sin, to rebel in iniquity, and to wallow in lust, what would be the use of such forgiveness? Wouldn't such forgiveness turn out to be a sweet poison, which would effectually destroy us? To be washed and still lie in the muck and mire, to be pronounced clean and still have leprosy would be the greatest mockery of mercy. What is the purpose of bringing the man out of his sepulcher if you leave him dead? Why lead him into the light if he is still blind?

We thank God that He who forgives our sins also heals our diseases. He who washes away the stains of the past also uplifts us from the foul ways of the present and keeps us from failing in the future. We must joyfully accept both repentance and the lessening of the seriousness or intensity of our current sin. The two cannot be separated. The promised inheritance is one and is indivisible and must not be parceled out. To divide the work of grace would be to cut the living child in two (1 Kings 3:25). Those who would permit this have no interest in it.

As you seek the Lord, I ask whether you would be satisfied with only one of these mercies. Would you be content if God forgave your sin and then allowed you to be as worldly and wicked as before? No! The born-again spirit is more afraid of sin itself than of the punishment that results from it. The cry of your heart will no longer be, "Who will deliver me from punishment?" but, *Wretched man that I am! Who will set me free from the body of this death?* (Romans 7:24). Since repentance is connected with a decrease in sin resulting from a desire proceeding from divine grace, and since it is necessary for the completeness of salvation and for holiness, you can be sure it will continue permanently.

Repentance and forgiveness are joined together in the experience of all true believers. There's never been a person who sincerely repented of sin with *believing* repentance who wasn't forgiven. On the other hand, there's never been a person forgiven who hasn't repented of his sin. I don't hesitate to say that beneath heaven there never was, is, or will be any sin washed away, unless the heart is led to repentance and faith in Christ at the same time. Hatred of sin and a sense of pardon come together into the soul and abide together while we live.

These two things act on and react to each other. The man who is forgiven therefore repents, and the man who repents is also most assuredly forgiven. But remember, forgiveness comes first and leads to repentance. As we sing in Joseph Hart's words:

*Law and terrors do but harden,*
*All the while they work alone;*
*But a sense of blood-bought pardon*
*Soon dissolves a heart of stone.*

When we're sure we are forgiven, then we abhor sin. And I suppose when faith grows into full assurance and we're certain beyond a doubt that the blood of Jesus has washed us whiter than snow, it's then that repentance reaches its greatest height. Repentance grows as faith grows. Don't make any mistake about it. Repentance isn't something marked by days and weeks. It's not a temporary penance to be over as fast as possible. No. It's the grace of a lifetime, like faith itself. God's little children repent, and so do the young men and the fathers (1 John 2:13). Repentance is the inseparable companion of faith. All the while as we walk by faith and not by sight, the tear of repentance glitters in the eye of faith. Repentance that doesn't come from faith in Jesus isn't true repentance, and it's not true faith in Jesus if it isn't tinged with repentance.

**When we're sure we are forgiven, then we abhor sin.**

Faith and repentance are vitally joined together. We repent in proportion to our faith in the forgiving love of Christ, and we rejoice in the fullness of the absolution which Jesus is honored to grant in proportion to our repentance and hatred of sin and evil. You will never value pardon unless you feel repentance, and you'll never taste the deepest draught of repentance until you know you are pardoned. This may seem strange, but it is true. The bitterness of repentance and the sweetness of pardon blend in the flavor of every gracious life and produce incomparable happiness.

These two covenant gifts mutually guarantee each other. If I know I repent, I know I am forgiven. How am I to know I'm forgiven except that I know that I've turned from my former sinful course? To be a believer is to be repentant. Faith and repentance are two spokes in the same wheel, two handles of the same plough. Repentance has been described as a heart broken because of sin and from sin. Similarly, it can be spoken of as a turning from sin and a returning to God. It is a change of mind of the most thorough and radical sort, and it is joined with sorrow for the past and a resolve to change in the future.

> *Repentance is to leave*
> *The sins we loved before;*
> *And show that we in earnest grieve,*
> *By doing so no more.*

When that is the case, we can be certain we are forgiven, because the Lord never made a heart to be broken because of sin and broken from sin, without pardoning it. On the other hand, if we are enjoying forgiveness through the blood of Jesus, and are justified by faith, and have peace with God through Jesus Christ our Lord, we know our repentance and faith are of the right sort.

Don't think of your repentance as the cause of your pardon but as the companion of it. Don't expect to be able to repent until you see the grace of our Lord Jesus, and His readiness to blot out your sin. Keep these blessed things in their proper places. View them in their relation to each other. They are the pillars of a saving experience. No man rightly comes to God unless he passes between the pillars of repentance and forgiveness. The rainbow of God's promised grace upon your heart is displayed in all its beauty when teardrops of repentance are shone upon by the light of full forgiveness. Repentance of sin and faith in divine pardon are woven together in the fabric of real conversion. By these demonstrations you'll know a believer for sure.

**Repentance of sin and faith in divine pardon are woven together in the fabric of real conversion.**

When we look again at the Scripture we've been meditating on, we see that forgiveness and repentance flow from the same source and are given by the same Savior. The Lord Jesus, in His glory, bestows both on the same people. You aren't going to find the forgiveness nor the repentance elsewhere. Jesus has both of them ready and is prepared to grant them now – to give them freely to all who will accept them from His hands.

Never forget that Jesus gives all we need for our salvation. It is extremely important that all who seek mercy should remember this. Faith is as much the gift of God as is the Savior on whom that faith relies. Repentance of sin is actually the work of grace – like making an atonement by which sin is blotted out. Salvation, from the beginning to the end, is of grace alone (Ephesians 2:8). Don't misunderstand me. It's not the Holy Spirit who repents. He has never done anything for which He should repent. If He could repent, it wouldn't be suitable for the situation, because we must repent of our own sin. If we don't, we aren't saved from its power.

It's also not the Lord Jesus Christ who repents. What would He repent of? It is we who must repent with the full approval of every faculty of our mind. The will, passions, and emotions all work together wholeheartedly in the blessed act of repentance of sin. Behind it all is the holy influence on our personal behavior, which melts the heart, produces shame and regret, and brings about a complete change. The Spirit of God enlightens us to see what sin is and makes it detestable in our eyes.

The Spirit of God also turns us toward holiness and makes us wholeheartedly appreciate, love, and desire it. In this way, the Holy Spirit motivates and leads us from stage to stage of sanctification. The Spirit of God *who is at work in you, both to will and to work for His good pleasure* (Philippians 2:13). Let us submit ourselves immediately to His good Spirit, so He can lead us to Jesus, who will freely give us the double blessing of repentance and forgiveness, according to the riches of His grace.

"BY GRACE YOU HAVE BEEN SAVED."

Chapter 14

# How Repentance Is Given

For this chapter, we will return to Acts 5:31: *He is the one whom God exalted to His right hand as a Prince and a Savior, to grant repentance to Israel, and forgiveness of sins.* Our Lord Jesus Christ has gone up to heaven so grace can come down to us. His glory is busy giving greater reception to His grace. The reason the Lord has taken a step upward is because of His plan to carry believing sinners up to heaven with Him. He is exalted on high to give repentance, and we will see this for ourselves if we remember a few great truths.

The work our Lord Jesus has done has made repentance possible, available, and acceptable. The law makes no mention of repentance, but says clearly, *The person who sins will die* (Ezekiel 18:20). If the Lord Jesus hadn't died and risen again and gone to the Father, what would repenting be worth? We might feel remorse with its distresses, but never repentance with its renewed hope. Repentance as a natural feeling only is an everyday obligation which deserves no great praise. It is generally so mingled with a selfish fear of punishment, that the kindest appraisal makes little of it. If Jesus hadn't intervened and worked out a wealth of merit, our tears of repentance wouldn't be much more than water spilled on the ground. Jesus is exalted on high in heaven, so through the moral goodness of His intercession, repentance can have a place before God. In this respect, He gives us repentance, because He puts repentance into a position of acceptance, which otherwise it never could have occupied.

When Jesus was exalted on high, the Spirit of God was poured out to work all necessary graces in us. The Holy Spirit creates repentance in us by supernaturally renewing our nature and taking away the heart of stone out of our flesh (Ezekiel 36:26). Don't sit there straining to muster unattainable tears. Repentance doesn't come from an unwilling nature but from free and sovereign grace. Don't go to your bedroom to strike your breast in an attempt to call up feelings which aren't there in a heart of stone. Rather, go to Calvary and see how Jesus died. Look up to the hills from which your help comes (Psalm 121:1). The Holy Spirit has come purposely to overshadow men's spirits and produce repentance within them, even as He once brought forth order out of chaos. Breathe your prayer to Him, "Blessed Spirit, dwell with me. Make me tender and humble of heart, so I can hate

> Make me tender and humble of heart, so I can hate sin and sincerely repent of it.

sin and sincerely repent of it." He will hear your cry and answer you.

Remember that when our Lord Jesus was exalted, He not only gave us repentance by sending forth the Holy Spirit, but He also consecrated all the works of nature and of providence to attain our salvation. So any of these can call us to repentance, whether they crow like Peter's rooster or shake the prison like the jailer's earthquake (Acts 16:26). From the right hand of God, our Lord Jesus rules all things here on earth and makes them work together for the salvation of His redeemed. He uses both the bitter and the sweet, trials and joys, so He can produce a better mind in sinners toward their God.

Be thankful for God's timely preparation of future events which make you poor, or sick, or sad, because by all this Jesus works the life of your spirit and turns you to Himself. The Lord's mercy often rides to the door of our hearts on the black horse of affliction. Jesus uses the whole range of our experiences to wean us from this world and to woo us to heaven. Christ is exalted to the throne of heaven and earth in order that, by the courses of action of His providence, He can subdue hard hearts and bring them the gracious softening of repentance.

More to the point, He is at work right now by all His whispers in the conscience, by His inspired Word, by those of us who speak the message of the Bible, and by praying friends and sincere hearts. He can send a word to you which will strike your rocky heart as with the rod of Moses and cause streams of repentance to flow forth (Exodus 17:6). From the Holy Scripture, He can bring some heartbreaking text to your mind which will overcome you right away. He can mysteriously soften your heart, and when you least expect it cause a holy frame of mind to steal over you.

Be sure of this: Jesus, who has gone into His glory and has been raised into all the splendor and majesty of God, has abundant ways of working repentance in those to whom He grants forgiveness. Even now, He is waiting to give repentance to you. Ask Him for it now.

Take notice of how much comfort this repentance from the Lord Jesus Christ gives to the most unlikely people in the world. *He is the one whom God exalted to His right hand as a Prince and a Savior, to grant repentance to Israel, and forgiveness of sins* (Acts 5:31). To Israel! In the days when the apostles spoke like this, Israel was the nation which had sinned most grossly against light and love, by daring to say, *His blood shall be on us and on our children* (Matthew 27:25). Yet Jesus is raised to a position to give them repentance. What a marvel of grace.

If you've been brought up in the brightest of Christian light and have still rejected it, there is still hope. If you have sinned against conscience and against the Holy Spirit, and against the love of Jesus, there is still room for repentance. Though you may be as hard-hearted and unbelieving as Israel of old, softening of your heart may still come to you, since Jesus is exalted and clothed with boundless power. For those who have gone deep into sin and sinned the worst, the Lord Jesus is still able to give you repentance and forgiveness of sins.

I'm happy to have such a full gospel to proclaim, and you are blessed to be allowed to read it.

The hearts of the children of Israel had grown hard as stone. Martin Luther used to think it impossible to convert a Jew. While we don't agree with him in this, we must admit that the children of Israel have been exceedingly obstinate in their rejection of the Savior over the centuries. Rightly did the Lord say to the Jews, *I told you, and you do not believe* (John 10:25). *He came to His own, and those who were His own did not receive Him* (John 1:11). Yet our Lord Jesus is exalted on behalf of Israel for the giving of repentance and forgiveness. But many Gentiles have a similarly stubborn heart, which has stood against the Lord Jesus for years, yet in such a heart our Lord can still work repentance. When this happens, you may join your voice with that of William Hone after he yielded to divine love. While he was once a stout-hearted unbeliever, once his heart was subdued by sovereign grace, he wrote:

> *The proudest heart that ever beat*
> *Hath been subdued in me;*
> *The wildest will that ever rose,*
> *To scorn Thy cause and aid Thy foes,*
> *Is quelled, my God! by Thee.*
>
> *Thy will, and not my will be done,*
> *My heart be ever Thine;*
> *Confessing Thee, the mighty Word,*
> *I hail thee, Christ, my God, my Lord,*
> *And make Thy name my sign.*

The Lord can give repentance to the most unlikely, turning lions into lambs, and ravens into doves. Let's look to Him so this great change can be worked in us. Without a doubt, contemplating the death of Christ is one of the surest and speediest ways of being persuaded to repent. Don't sit down and try to pump up feelings of repentance from the dry well of corrupt nature. You can't force your soul into the gracious state of repentance. Instead, take your heart to Him who understands it and pray, "Lord, cleanse it. Lord, renew it. Lord, work repentance in it."

The more you try to produce repentant emotions on your own, the more you'll be disappointed. But if you think – with faith – of Jesus dying for you, repentance will burst forth. Meditate on the Lord's shedding His heart's blood out of love for you. Consider the agony and bloody sweat – the cross and the passion. As you do, He who bore all this grief will look at you, and with that look He will do for you what He did for Peter when he wept bitterly (Luke 22:62). He who died for you can, by His gracious Spirit, make you die to sin. He has gone into glory on your behalf and can draw your soul to follow after Him – away from evil and toward holiness.

I want to leave this one thought with you. Don't look beneath the ice to find fire, and don't hope in your own natural heart to find repentance. Look to the living One for life. Look to Jesus for all you need. Never seek elsewhere for any part of the love Jesus bestows, but remember, Christ is all.

Chapter 15

# The Fear of Final Falling

A dark fear haunts the minds of many coming to Christ. They fear they won't persevere to the end. I've heard one seeking salvation say, "Once I cast my soul upon Jesus, what if I'm drawn back into the penalty of hell after all? I've had good feelings before and they've died away. My goodness has been like the early dew. It came on quickly, lasted for a time, promised much, and then vanished."

I believe this fear is often the indicator of the fact that some people who have been afraid to trust Christ for all time and for all eternity have failed because they had a temporary faith, which never went far enough to save them. They set out trusting Jesus to a degree, but still looked to themselves for continuance and perseverance in living a godly life. Because they didn't put their faith in Christ alone, as a natural consequence, they turned back before long.

If we trust in our own ability to hold on, we will fail. Even though we rest in Jesus for our salvation, we will fail if we also try to place trust in self for anything. No chain is stronger than its weakest link. If Jesus is our hope for everything, except one thing, we will utterly fail, because in that one thing we'll come to nothing.

I have no doubt that this faulty thinking about the perseverance of the saints has prevented the perseverance of many who did run well. What hindered them? What stopped them from continuing to run? They trusted in themselves for that running and so they stopped short. **Beware of mixing even a little of self with the mortar with which you build,** or you'll make it untempered mortar, and the stones won't hold together. If you look to Christ at the start, beware that you don't look to yourself to complete Christ's work in you. He is the Alpha (beginning). See to it that you trust Him as the Omega (end) also. If you begin in the Spirit, you must not hope to be made perfect by the flesh. Begin as if you mean to go on, and go on as you began. Let the Lord be all in all to you. Pray that God the Holy Spirit will make it very clear where the strength must come from for us to persevere until the day of our Lord's appearing.

Here is what Paul once said about this subject when he wrote to the Corinthians: *who will also confirm you to the end, blameless in the day of our Lord Jesus Christ. God is faithful, through whom you were called into fellowship with His Son, Jesus Christ our Lord* (1 Corinthians 1:8-9).

This language silently admits a great need by telling us how it is provided for. Wherever the Lord makes a provision, we can be sure there is a need for it, since no superfluities hinder the covenant of grace. Golden shields hung in Solomon's courts, which were never used, but there's no such thing in the armory of God. What God has provided we will surely need. Between now and the completion of all things, every one of God's promises and every provision of the covenant of grace will be used.

The urgent need of the believing soul is confirmation, continuance, final perseverance, and preservation to the end. This is the great necessity of the most advanced believers, as we see when Paul wrote to believers at Corinth who were considered knowledgeable thinkers, of whom he could say, *I thank my God always concerning you for the grace of God which was given you in Christ Jesus* (1 Corinthians 1:4). It is such people who most assuredly feel they need new grace daily if they are to hold on, hold out, and succeed as conquerors in the end.

If you weren't a believer, you would have no grace and wouldn't feel the need for more grace; but because you are a believer, you feel the daily demands of the spiritual life. A marble statue requires no food, but the living man hungers and thirsts. He rejoices that his bread and water is certain or he would faint along the way. The believer's personal needs make it inevitable that he should draw from the great source of all each day, because if he couldn't resort to his God, what would he do?

This is true of the most gifted believers – of those people at Corinth who were enriched *in all speech and all knowledge* (1 Corinthians 1:5). They needed to be confirmed to the end or their gifts and attainments would turn out to be their ruin. If we spoke in the languages of men and angels but didn't receive fresh grace, where would we be? If we gained more and more experience until we became leaders in the church – if we were taught by God to understand all mysteries – still we couldn't live a single day without the divine life flowing into us from Christ, our covenant Head. How could we hope to hold on for a single hour, to say nothing of a lifetime, unless the Lord held on to us? *He who began a good work in you will perfect it until the day of Christ Jesus* (Philippians 1:6), or it will prove a painful failure.

This great necessity arises to a great extent from within ourselves. Some harbor a painful fear that they won't persevere in grace, because they know their own faithlessness. Related to general character, some people are unstable. Some are even-tempered by nature, but others are naturally unpredictable and hot-tempered. Like butterflies, they flit from flower to flower, until they visit all the beauties of the garden and settle on none of them. They are never in one place long enough to do any good, not even in their job or in their academic pursuits. Such people may be afraid that ten, twenty, thirty, forty, perhaps fifty years of continuous spiritual watchfulness will be too much for them. As a result, we see people joining one church after another, until they can recite the thirty-two points and quarter-points of the magnetic compass both clockwise and anticlockwise. Such people have double the need to pray that they can be divinely established and made not only steadfast but also unmovable. Otherwise they won't be found *always abounding in the work of the Lord* (1 Corinthians 15:58).

All of us, even if we have no deep-seated temptation to fickleness, once we are born again of God, must recognize our own weakness. In any single day, you will find enough to make you stumble. If you desire to walk in perfect holiness, as I trust you do, you must set a high standard regarding what a Christian should be. For most of us, before the breakfast dishes are cleared from the table, we've displayed enough foolishness to be ashamed of ourselves.

> In any single day, you will find enough to make you stumble.

If we shut ourselves up in the lonely cell of a hermit, temptation would still follow us, because as long as we can't escape from ourselves, we can't escape from the pull of sin. Within our hearts, there is that which should make us watchful and humble before God. If He doesn't strengthen us, we are so weak that we'll stumble and fall spiritually, not because we are overcome by an enemy, but by our own carelessness. Lord, be our strength, because we are weakness itself.

Besides that, there is the weariness which comes with a long life. When we begin our Christian life and profess our faith to others, we mount up with wings like eagles. As we grow in Him, we run without weariness, but it is on our best and truest days that we walk without fainting (Isaiah 40:31). Our pace may seem slower, but it is more useful and better sustained. I pray to God that the energy of our youth will continue with us when it comes to the energy of the Spirit and not just the excitement of proud flesh.

He who has walked on the road to heaven a long time finds there's good reason why it was promised that his shoes would be iron and brass (Deuteronomy 33:25), because the road is rough. He has discovered Hills of Difficulty and Valleys of Humiliation; that there is a Vale of Death Shade, and, worse still, a Vanity Fair – and all these are to be traveled. If there are to be Delectable Mountains (and, thank God, there are), there are also Doubting Castles of Despair, the inside of which pilgrims have too often seen[6]. Considering all things, those who hold out to the end in the way of holiness will be *men who are a symbol* (Zechariah 3:8).

"O world of wonders, I can say no less."[7] The days of a Christian's life are like many large, colorless diamonds of mercy threaded on the golden string of divine faithfulness. In heaven, we will tell angels, principalities, and powers of the unsearchable riches of Christ which were spent on us and enjoyed by us while here on earth. We've been kept alive on the brink of death. Our spiritual life has been a flame burning in the midst of the sea, a stone suspended in the air. It will amaze the universe to see us enter the pearly gates, blameless

---

6    References to John Bunyan's *The Pilgrim's Progress.*
7    Ibid.

in the day of our Lord Jesus Christ. We ought to be full of thankful wonder, if we are kept for a time, and I believe we are (John 6:39).

If this was all, we'd have enough cause for anxiety, but there's much more. We have to think about this world we live in. It's a howling wilderness to many of God's people. Some of us are greatly indulged in God's providence, but others have a serious fight of it. Some of us begin our day with prayer and often hear the voice of holy song fill our houses, but many good **The world is no friend to grace.** people scarcely rise from their knees in the morning before they are greeted with profanity. They go out to work and are aggravated with filthy conversation all day long. Can you even walk down the streets without being assaulted with foul language?

The world is no friend to grace. The best we can do with this world is to get through it as quickly as we can, because while we are here, we live in an enemy's country. A robber lurks in every bush. We need to travel everywhere with a drawn sword in our hand, or at least have that weapon called all-prayer always at our side because we must struggle for every inch of our way. Make no mistake about this, or you will be rudely shaken out of your warm delusion. God, help us and validate our spiritual birth to the end, or where will we be?

True faith is supernatural at its beginning, super- natural in its continuance, and supernatural at its close. It is the work of God from beginning to end. There's still a great need for the hand of the Lord to be outstretched. It's a need you feel now, and I'm glad you feel it. That means you will look to the Lord for your own preservation now. He alone is able to keep us from failing and to glorify us with His Son.

# Chapter 16

# Spiritual Confirmation

I want you to notice the security Paul confidently expected for all the saints. He says, *who will also confirm you to the end, blameless in the day of our Lord Jesus Christ* (1 Corinthians 1:8). This kind of confirmation is to be desired above all things. It supposes souls are right and proposes to confirm them in the right. It would be awful to confirm a man in the ways of sin and error. Think of a confirmed drunkard, or a confirmed thief, or a confirmed liar. It would be a deplorable thing for a man to be confirmed in unbelief and ungodliness.

Spiritual confirmation can only be enjoyed by those who have already received the grace of God. It is the work of the Holy Spirit. He who gives faith strengthens and establishes it. He who kindles love in us preserves it and increases its flame. What He makes us to know by His first teaching, the good Spirit, with further instruction, causes us to know with greater clearness and certainty.

Holy acts are established until they become habits, and holy feelings are validated until they become long-lasting. Experience and practice confirm our beliefs and our resolutions, in the same way the tree is helped to root by the soft showers and the rough winds. Both our joys and our sorrows, our successes and our failures are sanctified to the very same end. The mind is instructed and gathers reasons for persevering in the good way through its growing knowledge. The heart is comforted and made to cling more closely to the consoling truth. The grip grows tighter, the pace grows certain, and the believer becomes more solid and substantial.

This is more than mere natural growth. It is a distinct work of conversion by the Spirit. The Lord gives it to those who rely on Him for eternal life. By His inward working, He delivers us from being *uncontrolled as water* (Genesis 49:4) and causes us to be rooted and grounded in Him. It is a part of the method by which He saves us – this building us up into Christ Jesus and causing us to abide in Him. As a believer, you can look for this daily, and you won't be disappointed. As you place your trust in Him, He will make you to be like a tree planted by rivers of waters, so preserved that even your leaf won't wither (Psalm 1:3).

A confirmed Christian is a strength to the church. He is a comfort to the sorrowful and a help to the weak. Wouldn't you like to be such a Christian? Confirmed believers are pillars in the house of God who aren't carried away by every wind of doctrine, or overthrown

by sudden temptation (Ephesians 4:14). They are a
great support to others and act like anchors in times
of church trouble. If you are just beginning your life in
Christ, you hardly dare to hope you will become like
them, but lay that fear aside, because the good Lord
will work in you as well as in them. While you're just
a "babe" in Christ now, one of these days you will be a
"father" in the church. Hope for this as a gift of grace
and not as something you've earned through works or
as the product of your own efforts.

The inspired apostle Paul speaks of these people as
being confirmed unto the end. He expected the grace
of God to preserve them personally to the end of their
lives, or until the return of the
Lord Jesus. In reality, he expected
the whole church of God in every
place and through all time to keep
and persevere until the Lord Jesus

**The work of grace
in the soul isn't a
superficial reformation.**

returned as the Bridegroom to celebrate the wedding
feast with his perfected bride – the church. All who are
in Christ will be confirmed in Him until that illustri-
ous day. Didn't Jesus Himself say, *because I live, you
will live also*? (John 14:19). He also said, *I give eternal
life to them, and they will never perish; and no one will
snatch them out of My hand* (John 10:28). *He who began
a good work in you will perfect it until the day of Christ
Jesus* (Philippians 1:6).

The work of grace in the soul isn't a superficial reformation. The life implanted at the new birth comes
from a living and incorruptible seed, which lives and
abides forever (1 Peter 1:23). The promises of God

made to believers aren't temporary, but their fulfilment involves the believer holding his way until he comes to endless glory. *The righteous will hold to his way* (Job 17:9). This is possible because we are kept by the power of God, through faith unto salvation, not as the result of our own merit or strength, but as a gift of free and undeserved approval for those who are *kept for Jesus Christ* (Jude 1). Jesus will lose none of the sheep of His fold. Not a single member of His body will die spiritually. No gem of His treasure will be missing in the day when He makes up His jewels. The salvation which is received by faith isn't a thing we work for over months and years, because our Lord Jesus has already obtained eternal salvation for us. Since it is eternal, that means it can't come to an end.

Paul also declares his expectation that the Corinthian saints would be confirmed to the end blameless (1 Corinthians 1:8). This blamelessness is a precious part of our being kept in Him. To be kept holy is more than just being kept safe. It is dreadful when you see religious people blundering from one dishonor into another because they haven't believed in the power of our Lord to make them blameless. Even the lives of some professing Christians are a series of stumbles. They never quite fall down, but they are seldom on their feet. This isn't fitting for a believer who is invited to walk with God. By faith he can reach toward holiness with a steady tenacity, and he ought to do just that. The Lord is able not only to save us from hell but also to keep us from falling.

We don't need to yield to temptation. Isn't it written

that *sin shall not be master over you* (Romans 6:14)? The Lord is able to keep the feet of His saints from stumbling, and He will do it if we will trust Him to do so. We don't need to defile our garments, because by His grace we can keep them unspotted from the world. We are bound to do this, for without holiness no one will see the Lord (Hebrews 12:14). The apostle prophesied for these believers the very thing he wants us to

> The Lord is able to keep the feet of His saints from stumbling, and He will do it if we will trust Him to do so.

seek after – that we can be preserved, *holy and blameless and beyond reproach* (Colossians 1:22). The Lord's own are unimpeachable.

God grant that in that last great day we can stand clear of all charges, so no one in the whole universe can dare to challenge our claim to be the redeemed of the Lord. We have failures and infirmities to mourn over, but these aren't the kind of faults which would prove us to be outside of Christ. We will be clear of ongoing, unrepentant hypocrisy, deceit, hatred, immorality, and delight in sin, because these would be fatal charges.

Despite our failings, the Holy Spirit can work a spotless character in us before men, so that, like Daniel, we will provide no occasion for people to accuse us, except in the matter of our faith. Multitudes of godly men and women have exhibited lives so transparent, so thoroughly consistent, that no one could speak against them. Regarding such believers today, the Lord will be able to say what He said about Job when Satan stood before Him: *Have you considered My servant Job? For there is no one like him on the earth, a blameless and upright man, fearing God and turning away from evil?* (Job 1:8).

This is what you must look for at the Lord's hands. This is the triumph of the saints – to continue to follow the Lamb wherever He goes and to maintain our integrity before the living God. May we never turn aside into corrupt ways and give cause to the adversary to speak reproachfully of God or the Holy Spirit. For it is written of the true believer that *he who was born of God keeps him, and the evil one does not touch him* (1 John 5:18). May the same thing be written concerning us.

> Even if you lived deep in sin in the past, the Lord can totally deliver you from the power of former habits and make you an example of virtue.

If you are just beginning in the divine life, the Lord can give you an irreproachable character. Even if you lived deep in sin in the past, the Lord can totally deliver you from the power of former habits and make you an example of virtue. He cannot only make you moral, but He can also make you abhor every false way and follow after all that is godly. Don't doubt it. The chief of sinners doesn't need to be a bit behind the purest believer. Believe this and according to your faith it will be done for you.

Oh, what a joy it will be to be found blameless in the day of judgment. We aren't mistaken when we join in that wonderful hymn "Jesus, Thy Blood and Righteousness"[8] and sing:

> *Bold shall I stand in that great day,*
> *For who ought to my charge shall lay?*
> *While, through Thy blood, absolved I am*
> *From sin's tremendous curse and shame?*

What a delight it will be to enjoy that bold courage, when heaven and earth flee from the face of the judge of all. This bliss will be the portion of everyone who looks to the grace of God in Christ Jesus and nothing else, and who in that sanctified strength wages continual war with all sin.

---

8    Charles B. Snepp, ed., *Songs of Grace and Glory for Private, Family, and Public Worship* (London: W. Hunt & Co., 1872).

## Chapter 17

# Why Saints Persevere

We have already seen the hope which filled the heart of the apostle Paul concerning the Corinthian brothers to be a comfort to those who trembled regarding their future. But why was it that he believed that the brethren would be confirmed – strengthened and established – to the end?

If you look closely at 1 Corinthians 1:9, you will notice he gives his reasons. Here they are:

> *God is faithful, through whom you were called into fellowship with His Son, Jesus Christ our Lord.*

The apostle doesn't say, "You are faithful." Unfortunately, the faithfulness of humans is a very unreliable matter. It's just futility.

He doesn't say, "You have faithful ministers to lead and guide you, and therefore I trust you will be safe."

No. If we are to be kept by men, we will only be poorly kept. He says, *God is faithful.* If we are found faithful, it will be because God is faithful, not because of another person. The whole burden of our salvation must rest on the faithfulness of our God, because the matter hinges on this glorious attribute of God.

We are as unpredictable as the wind, frail as a spider's web, and weak as water. We can place no dependence on our natural qualities or our spiritual achievements, *He* [God] *remains faithful* (2 Timothy 2:13). He is faithful in His love *with . . . no variation or shifting shadow* (James 1:17). He is faithful to His purpose. He doesn't begin a work and then leave it undone (Philippians 1:6). He is faithful to His relationships. As a Father, He will not renounce His children. As a friend, He won't deny His people. As the Creator, He will not forsake the work of His hands. He is faithful to His promises and will never allow one of them to fail a single believer. He is faithful to His covenant, which He has made with us in Christ Jesus and ratified with the blood of His sacrifice. He is faithful to His Son, and will not allow His precious blood to be spilled in vain. He is faithful to His people to whom He has promised eternal life and from whom He will not turn away.

> God is faithful to His relationships.

This faithfulness of God is the foundation and cornerstone of our hope of final perseverance. True believers will press on in holiness, because God perseveres in grace. He continues to bless, and so believers continue in being blessed. He continues to keep His people, and therefore they continue to keep His commandments.

This is good solid ground to rest on. Along these lines, it is free favor and infinite mercy which usher in the dawn of salvation, and the same sweet bells sound melodiously through the whole day of grace.

The only reasons for hoping that we will be confirmed and found blameless in the end are found in our God, and in Him these reasons are exceedingly abundant. They lie first in what God has done. He has gone so far in blessing us that it isn't possible for Him to run back. Paul reminds us that He has *called [us] into fellowship with his Son, Jesus Christ our Lord* (1 Corinthians 1:9). If He called us, then the call can't be reversed, because *the gifts and the calling of God are irrevocable* (Romans 11:29). The Lord never turns from the powerful call of His grace.

*Whom He called, He also justified; and these whom He justified, He also glorified* (Romans 8:30). This is the unchanging rule of God's divine procedure. A familiar call in Scripture says, *Many are called, but few are chosen* (Matthew 22:14), but what we're talking about now is something else – another kind of call, which promises special love and requires the possession of that to which we are called. With the called one in this case, like with Abraham's seed, the Lord has said, *You whom I have taken from the ends of the earth, and called from its remotest parts and said to you, You are My servant, I have chosen you and not rejected you* (Isaiah 41:9).

We see strong reasons for our preservation and future glory in what the Lord has done. The Lord has called us into the fellowship of His Son Jesus Christ. Carefully consider what this means. It means we are called into partnership with Jesus Christ. If you are in fact called by divine grace, you have come into fellowship with the Lord Jesus Christ, as a joint owner with Him in all things. From now on, you are one with Him in the sight of the Most High.

The Lord Jesus carried your sins in His own body on the cross. With this act, He was made a curse for you and at the same time He became your righteousness. As a result, you're justified in Him. You are Christ's and Christ is yours. In the same way Adam stood for his descendants, Jesus stands for all who are in Him. As husband and wife are one, so is Jesus one with all united to Him by faith – one by a conjugal union which can never be broken.

More than this, believers are members of the body of Christ and so are one with Him by a loving, living, lasting union. God has called us into this union, this fellowship, this partnership, and by this very fact, He has given us the token and pledge of our being confirmed to the end. If we were to be considered apart from Christ, we would be poor perishable individuals, soon carried away to eternal destruction. But when we are one with Jesus, we are made partakers of His nature and endowed with His immortal life. Our destiny is linked with our Lord's, and until He can be destroyed, it isn't possible for us to perish.

Dwell on this partnership with the Son of God – this partnership to which you have been called – because all your hope lies there. Since you are firmly in a partnership with Him, you can never be poor while Jesus is rich. Poverty can never torment you, since you are a joint proprietor with Him who is possessor of heaven and earth. You can never fail, because even though one of the partners in the firm is poor, utterly bankrupt, and unable to pay even a small amount of his hefty debts, the other partner is still inconceivably, inexhaustibly rich. In such a partnership, you are raised above the unhappiness of the times, the changes of the future, and the shock of the end of all things. The Lord has called you into the fellowship of His Son Jesus Christ, and by that deed He has put you into the place of unfailing protection.

If you are indeed a believer, you are one with Jesus and therefore secure. Do you see the truth in this? You must be confirmed as His to the end, until the day you meet Him, if you've really been made one with Jesus by the irrevocable act of God.

Then you, the believing sinner, are in the same boat with Jesus and unless Jesus sinks, the believer never will drown. Jesus has taken His redeemed into such a relationship with Himself, that He must first be beaten, overcome, and dishonored, lest the least of His purchased ones might be injured. His name is at the head of the firm, and until it can be dishonored, we are secure against all dread of failure.

> We can move forward with great confidence into the unknown future, because we are linked eternally with Jesus.

As a result, we can move forward with great confidence into the unknown future, because we are linked eternally with Jesus. If the people of the world ask, *Who is this coming up from the wilderness leaning on her beloved?* (Song of Solomon 8:5), we will joyfully confess that we lean on Jesus and that we intend to lean on Him more and more. Our faithful God is an ever-flowing well of delight and our fellowship with the Son of God is a river full of joy. Knowing these glorious things, we can't be discouraged. No. We rather cry with the apostle, *Who will separate us from the love of Christ?* (Romans 8:35).

# Conclusion

If you haven't followed me step by step as you've read the pages of this book, then I'm truly sorry. Reading a book is of little value unless the truths which pass before the mind are grasped, adopted, and practically applied. It's like a person who sees plenty of food in a store and still remains hungry, because they personally don't eat any of it. If this is how it is for you regarding the reading of this book, it's all in vain that you and I have met through the pages of this book, unless you've actually accepted Christ Jesus, my Lord.

On my part, there's a distinct desire to help you spiritually and eternally. I've done my best to accomplish this, and I've longed to win that privilege. I was thinking of you when I wrote this page, and I laid down my pen and fervently bowed in prayer for everyone who would read it. It is my firm conviction that great numbers of readers will be blessed, and it pains me if

I haven't been able to reach you in this way. If that is the case, I must ask, why would you refuse?

If you don't desire the excellent blessing I've brought to you, at least be fair and admit that the blame for your final fate will not lie at my door. When the two of us meet before the great white throne, you won't be able to blame me for idly using the attention you gave me while reading my little book. God knows that I wrote each line for your eternal good. I now take you by the hand in spirit with a firm grip. Do you feel my brotherly grasp? Tears fill my eyes as I look at you and say, "Why will you die? Won't you give your soul a thought? Will you choose to perish spiritually through sheer carelessness? Please don't do this. Weigh these serious matters and make sure to choose for eternity. Don't refuse Jesus, His love, His blood, His salvation. Why would you do that? Can you really do it? I plead with you not to turn away from your Redeemer."

On the other hand, if my prayers are heard and you've been led to trust the Lord Jesus and receive from Him salvation by grace, then keep this doctrine and this way of living. Let Jesus be your all in all and live and move in free grace alone. There's no other life like the life of someone who lives in the favor of God. To receive all this as a free gift safeguards the mind from self-righteous pride and from self-accusing despair. It makes the heart grow warm with grateful love, and, in this way, it creates a feeling in the soul which is infinitely more acceptable to God than anything that can possibly come of mindless fear.

Those who hope to be saved by trying to do their

best know nothing of that radiant commitment, that blessed warmth and devout joy in God which come with salvation freely given according to the grace of God. The foolish spirit of self-salvation is no match when compared to the joyous spirit of adoption. There's more real benefit in the smallest feeling of faith than in all the tugging of legal promises or all the weary works of devotees who plan to climb to heaven by sequences of ceremonies. Faith is spiritual, and God who is a spirit delights in it for that reason.

> Look first to the inner man and to the spiritual, and the rest will follow in due course.

Years of saying prayers, going to church or chapel, and participating in ceremonies and performances may only be an abomination in the sight of God. But a glance from the eye of true faith is spiritual and dear to Him. *For such people the Father seeks to be His worshipers* (John 4:23). Look first to the inner man and to the spiritual, and the rest will follow in due course.

If you are saved, be on the watch for the souls that are not. Your own heart won't prosper unless it is filled with intense concern for others. The life of your soul lies in faith. Its health lies in love. He who doesn't long to lead others to Jesus has never been under the influence of His love. Get to the work of the Lord – the work of love. Begin at home. Next, visit your neighbors. Tell the people of the village or who live on the street on which you live. Scatter the Word of the Lord like seed, wherever your hand can reach.

Dear reader, meet me in heaven. Don't choose to go down to hell. There is no coming back from that place of misery. Why do you wish to enter the way of death when heaven's gate is open before you? Don't refuse the free pardon, the full salvation which Jesus grants to all who trust Him. Don't hesitate or delay. You have had enough time to decide. It's time for action. Believe in Jesus now with an immediate and complete determination. Take words with you and come to your Lord today, for it may be now or never. Be sure. Let it be NOW, because it would be horrible if it were to be never.

Again I tell you – meet me in heaven.

# About the Author

Charles Haddon (C. H.) Spurgeon (1834-1892) was a British Baptist preacher. He started preaching at age 19, and quickly became famous. He is still known as the "Prince of Preachers," and frequently had more than 10,000 people present to hear him preach at the Metropolitan Tabernacle in London. His sermons were printed in newspapers, translated into many languages, and published in many books.